AF472361

As It Is In Heaven

Jeanne-Louise Viljoen

WestBow Press books may be ordered through booksellers or by contacting:

WestBow Press
A Division of Thomas Nelson & Zondervan
1663 Liberty Drive
Bloomington, IN 47403
www.westbowpress.com
1 (866) 928-1240

ISBN: 978-1-4908-6993-3 (sc)
ISBN: 978-1-4908-6994-0 (hc)
ISBN: 978-1-4908-6992-6 (e)

Library of Congress Control Number: 2015902363

Print information available on the last page.

WestBow Press rev. date: 03/26/2015

Contents

PART 2: PRACTICAL REVELATION

Dedication

Firstly, I dedicate this work to Almighty God, His precious Son Jesus Christ and my counselor the Holy Spirit. Without them I would not have been able to convey the experience of heaven, the capability of true transformation in a person's life, and the splendor of the Trinity (Father, Son, and Holy Spirit). I give God all the praise and glory for giving me the privilege to have been a part of the journey of this book. Looking back on this memorable endeavour, I realise the words put to paper are alive with power, revelation, and blessing, to the eyes of those who will get to read it. These words may one day surpass my own life, but the anointing on this book will remain forever. It is all because of the grace of our Lord Jesus Christ.

To my precious parents, Jacques and Denise. Thank you for being such an encouragement throughout my life. God has been ever good to us as a family, supplying our every need, for every season. You were chosen by God's own hand to be my parents, who gave all of yourselves to my brother and I. Thank you. I love and appreciate you.

I also dedicate this work to my brother, Ernest and his lovely wife Loraine. The love you all have shown towards this project has provided me the confidence needed to complete this dream. You have believed in the potential that this book would bring love and hope into the world out there. You are so precious to me and so dearly loved.

Finally I dedicate this work to all my family and friends who helped shape my life. I especially think of those who are no longer here with us. Even though we are separated for a time, one day, I will rejoice once more when I look upon your faces, when I return home to God's country, called heaven.

> "I thank God, whom I serve, as my ancestors did, with a clear conscience, as night and day I constantly remember you in my prayers. Recalling your tears, I long to see you, so that I may be filled with joy" (2 Timothy 1:3-4).
>
> ***Jeanne-Louise Viljoen***

Acknowledgements

A very special thanks to Stephnie Botha, Lynette Mentor, and Walda Botha who dedicated their time and wonderful ideas to assist in the moulding of this beautiful work. Through the Lord's guidance and intervention, He sent the right people to assist in bringing this book into existence. Thank you, Lord.

To my dear friends Suzie, Freda, Dinah, Lisa, Denice and Jenny who spent time in prayer and support throughout the last two years, speaking and praying this work into existence.

A special thanks to Pastor Denice Campion, and my friend Louise, whom God used prophetically in the development of this work.

Lastly, to all my friends and family who I may not have mentioned by name. Thank you for your love and support. Thank you for being a part of my life.

Jeanne-Louise Viljoen

Introduction

Years had gone by, before I decided to share about the testimony of heaven and dying. The experience alone was overwhelming and difficult to express, especially in a world where people only believe in what they can see. The following Scripture, written by Paul, resonates with my own heart:

I will reluctantly tell you about visions and revelations from the Lord. I was caught up to the third heaven fourteen years ago. Whether I was in my body or out of my body, I don't know – only God knows. Yes only God knows whether I was in my body or outside my body. But I do know that I was caught up to paradise and heard things so astounding that they cannot be expressed in words, things no human is allowed to tell. (2 Corinthians 12: 1 – 4 NLT)

Similar to Paul's description here, some words do not exist to convey each and every one of the astonishing things I saw and experienced, – "things no human is allowed to tell." There are several conversations that cannot be shared, which remain between God and the person.

That experience is worth boasting about, but I'm not going to do it. I will boast only about my weaknesses…, because I don't want anyone to give me credit beyond what they can see in my life or hear in my message, even though I have received such wonderful revelations from God. (2 Corinthians 12: 5 – 6 NLT)

I love this part of the Scripture that Paul wrote. It reflects my heart regarding why I shared my story. The experience, in the end, is all about the Lord, His mercy, His love, and His power to bring us true freedom, peace, and life. The Lord allowed me to return and apply heaven, as a design for my own life here and now.

You will find Scriptures throughout this book. It is important to appreciate the truth in this experience, and how it reflects God's Word. The purpose of this work is to reveal how intertwined our lives are, here on earth, with our lives hereafter. It contains a lot of in-depth, soul-searching, life-changing and thought-provoking bits.

What made this book such a passionate project, is the fact that alongside the testimony, comes the lessons of living a lifestyle that reflect heaven in our every-day life. A lot of questions are addressed, such as death, life after death, the meaning your life has on earth, the impact you make on loved ones, where people go when they die, where God fits in, how the Holy Spirit functions both in heaven and on earth, our life's purpose, forgiveness, and changing lifestyles, - just to name a few.

The book is for everyone who wants to know about heaven, the love of God, those who are stuck in a rut, those who have experienced great trauma, and those who have lost loved ones. It is also for those who have struggled with sickness, suicide, anger, every form of addiction and sin. The list can go on. "As it is in Heaven" is meant for every person ever born into this broken world.

Enjoy this journey that you are about to embark on. Take time to soak in each chapter. May this book reach your heart to reveal, touch, change, or direct you to the love and freedom of Jesus Christ. May you recognize how precious you are to Him.

Jeanne-Louise Viljoen

PART

Testimony

SECTION 1

The End of My Life

"Sometimes things need to end before they can truly start."

CHAPTER 1

In the Beginning

Growing up, I was very sure of what my future held.

"You need to lie still now, see? The doctor noticed a crack in one of your neck vertebrae on the X-ray. So if you move, you could break your neck, all right?" These were the worrying words of the now-concerned nurse who had been looking after me since I came in through casualty with my mom. These are probably some of the most frightening words a sixteen-year-old girl could hear from an emergency room nurse.

It was about 6:00 in the evening. Just a couple of hours ago, I was in full swing, playing first team tennis league. While waiting for my mixed-doubles partner to serve, I was struck with a hard blow to the back of my head, by a tennis ball. Next, I found myself waking up on the court with people splashing water over my face. By their concerned looks, I realized I must have passed out - for how long, I do not know. There was no way they would allow me to continue playing if there was the slightest possibility of a concussion. So I was taken to rest at the club-house. I noticed my mixed- doubles partner felt terrible. He was very quiet and worried. This was just an accident and could have happened to anyone.

After the day's game, members of the team took me directly home. My mom met the team members outside at the gate, and they started explaining to her what had happened to me. All present parties agreed that it would be a good idea to have me checked out at the hospital.

Mom rushed into the house to lock up and drive me over to the nearby hospital. We walked in, and I attempted to keep my mom calm by joking around with her. "*This can't be that serious*", I thought. At the front desk, we announced ourselves and explained the situation. The kind receptionist pointed us to the emergency room to see the doctor on duty.

Once the doctor was informed of the events that took place, I was asked to go through for some X-rays. I had never broken any bones before, so it was my first time to have X-rays taken. It was fairly painless.

Not long after, I was asked to rest on a bed in the trauma unit as we waited for the results. Mom and I were just chatting as usual. The doctor then appeared and asked my mom to come over to one side, – just out of earshot. I saw the startled look on my mom's face, and then the tears came. "*What is he saying to her? Why is Mom crying?*" While I contemplated this, the nurse came rushing over to me. She gently pushed me down into a lying position and placed a neck brace around my neck. "You need to lie still now, see? The doctor noticed a crack in one of your neck vertebrae on the X-ray. So if you move, you could break your neck, all right?"

I just went quiet. I stared at the ceiling, and my thoughts were flooded by images of me in a wheelchair. "*No, I won't give up. If it means I may need to learn to walk again I will do it, but this is not going to be my life.*" The tears were welling up at the back of my eyelids, but I needed to be strong for my mom's sake.

Memories of my life raced through my mind. As far back as age six, I was already able to hold a tennis racquet in my hand. "She has natural talent," was the comment of my very first coach, – at that time, I was barely able to see over the tennis net. Boy, could I swing a racquet. My parents did all they could to support my sport, especially because I loved the game so much.

Holidays and weekends were spent training and playing tournaments. My mom never missed a game. My dad supported me financially, as he was a very busy pharmacist. I knew my tennis playing was going to take me somewhere one day. I just couldn't see myself not playing. I was already at the provincial level and even dreaming of playing overseas.

The tennis training cultivated discipline, stamina, and courage. These qualities seemed to filter through everything I focused on, such as school-work, sports, and art. "Never give in. Never give up. Keep fighting back." Those were the words my mom encouraged me with before each match. However, the one most vital thing to master was my mind. On the tennis court, where you were on your own, you needed to fight your own battle. Every athlete knows that the biggest battle lies within the mind. The secret to winning the game was to know you were playing against yourself, more than your opponent. If you had the wrong mindset toward the game and yourself, you'd just handed the game over to the opposition. In all this, I also knew that God needed to be with me. I needed to draw my courage and strength from somewhere other than myself. Deep in my heart, I knew I was weak and sometimes lacked the needed courage and strength. Fear before a match was natural. As soon as I faced the fear and played through it, confidence and boldness would soon follow, – regardless of whether I was winning or losing.

That night though, I was faced with a different challenge, a much tougher challenge that could change my life. It would be my choice to live and fight back, or just slump into dismay and fear. "*Lord, I need to get through this. I cannot give up, whatever happens from here on out, I cannot give up.*" For the first time I felt afraid.

CHAPTER 2

Small Miracle

Do you believe in angels?

"*Where is my Dad*?" I looked around and found him standing beside my bed. He was very quiet through all this. Usually, he was the one speaking to the doctors, and finding out what was happening. Why was he just standing there with me?

As if he knew my thoughts, he turned to me and smiled, saying, "You are going to be fine." I felt at peace once those words reached my ears. Then I looked at my mom still speaking with the doctor. She seemed to be in silent shock as she listened to him.

"Dad, Mom seems to be taking this really hard. Won't you just go stand with her?" He smiled and then turned to go and join her and the doctors. To see my dad just standing there made me feel better in some way. Not long after that, the nurse came again and said that I was to go for a CAT scan. They needed to confirm what they saw on the X-ray.

After the final tests were done, I was sent home and asked to return to the doctor in three days' time for another X-ray. When we got home, my dad looked at the X-ray and then showed it to me. There was a clear crack in the one neck vertebrae. What made it stranger was the fact that

I was looking at my own neck. These X-rays were mine, not someone else's; that made it more real to me.

***

The next couple of nights, I slept on my back, not moving a muscle. During the day, I would sketch to keep my mind occupied. On Sunday morning, while my parents were out, I sat at the kitchen table, busy with the drawing I had started the day before. Then as clear as day, I heard a voice saying, "There is nothing wrong with your neck." That was it. Was I dreaming or imagining this voice? Was this God speaking to me? When my parents came back, I decided not to share this experience with them. What if they wouldn't understand, - especially my dad?

Then Monday came – day three. Mom drove me to the hospital after school. It was quiet in the car on the way there. Our thoughts were almost audible, "*What if the crack is still there?*"

The first thing that had to happen at the hospital was to have X-rays taken. The doctor had promised to fit me into his busy schedule. Within twenty minutes, the doctor invited us into his office. He was smiling. "The X-rays are clear. There is no crack visible. It must have been a shadow on the X-ray." My mom was visibly relieved, and we got out of there as fast as we possibly could.

We were both chatting, relieved at the results. The next day was school again, this time with no neck brace. How was I going to explain that? One day I had the neck brace, the next, I had none. My dad was also glad to hear the news later that evening.

***

About sixteen years later, I mentioned this experience to my mom while having coffee with her at her favourite coffee shop. When I mentioned the part about my dad standing at my bedside while the doctors spoke to her, she looked at me with a questioning look on her face.

"Jeanne, I was alone with you at the hospital. Remember, Dad was working that evening at the pharmacy. I had to call him to get authorization for all the tests, yes, but he wasn't there," she said gently. I looked at her with complete shock on my face. All this time I thought it was my dad who was there. When I thought back to my dad's body language and words, I realized this must have been an angel.

"Mom, I think it must have been an angel that came to stand with you and me?"

My mom had tears in her eyes, as this whole incident had left a deep scar on her life. I had never seen an angel before age sixteen. On that day at the hospital, I did, and what an encounter it was.

I'm sure I'm not the only person with such an encounter. Whether we have experienced the help of people, or angels, in our most desperate times, God really does care about all of us. He sends ever-present help in times of need.

> "God is our refuge and strength, an ever-present help in times of trouble" (Psalm 46:1 GW – God's Word Translation).

CHAPTER 3

Unexpected Setback

The dream was over.

Later, in the same year of my tennis incident, I went on a church youth camp. My parents made sure we were involved in church activities. They wanted us to grow up knowing the Lord. At age sixteen, at this youth camp, I rededicated my life and heart to Jesus Christ. I've always had a relationship with Jesus, but at the camp, I was encouraged to accept Him again. Personally I didn't mind, because I knew I loved God.

After the camp, my hunger to spend time in God's Word had increased. In my room, I would spend days praying and reading about the Lord. I loved every minute of it.

Sports had taught me discipline, endurance, and focus. With training, came results. I learned how to deal with failure, - to get up and keep trying. In a way, my sports had helped me cultivate a strong relationship with God.

In my seventeenth year, my tennis improved tremendously, while my academics remained strong. I was currently ranked number fourteen on the South African tennis rankings. One day, I received a letter from Tennis South Africa. They were organizing an ITF tour to England and invited me to participate. We would be playing matches against different nations in different areas of England. The tour offered the opportunity for each participant to gain experience in playing tennis on all kinds of surfaces - shale, clay, grass, and hard court.

My dad was able to sponsor the trip for me. I was very grateful to him. In all my life, my parents planned for our futures. They made sure that my brother and I would be able to go to university some day. They also supported our other interests we desired to follow.

The ITF tour turned out to be amazing. On my return to South Africa, my coach and I decided to pursue the professional world of tennis. My training increased, as we prepared for the pro-tours. One tournament after another had become preparation for my new path, the fulfilling of a life-long dream.

***

The final year of high school had arrived. I had an excitement about finishing school, and heading out into the world of pro-tennis. Even though I would still have to attend university, my focal point was tennis.

Around mid-year, I picked up a cold, followed by laryngitis. My mom took me to a doctor to get some medication. Apart from the laryngitis, I was fine. The doctor recommended some antibiotic, and sent me home. A couple of weeks later, I noticed that I had lost my appetite. My body seemed tired, but I didn't think anything of it. Once my mom noticed my lack of appetite, she realized I needed to go see our local doctor. My dad was under the impression I had flu, and thought my mom was only fussing about noting.

The very next day, after school, we were at the doctor. He took one look at me and immediately requested blood tests. Then he said, "I am pretty sure you have jaundice. We just need to determine which one, and how serious it is. However, let us first get you vaccinated. This includes all the people you were in contact with in the last 24 hours." With a blank expression on her face, my mom stared at him, before saying, "That would be everyone she came into contact with at her school ..."

Then the doctor added, "And of course you and her family." This did not sound like good news, but the situation was about to get a lot worse.

***

Over the next two months, my health deteriorated. My liver stopped functioning and my body became toxic. It was decided that, for the time being, I would be monitored at home. I was on liver medication, and a diet, consisting of some kind of toast, one slice, three times a day. Most of my time was spent sleeping.

Days and nights blurred together as I had become more ill. It was up to my body to fight the virus. For two months, a friend from school would drop-off homework assignments, which my mom completed for me in the mean while.

One night, during this illness, I had a dream. The Lord showed me how sick and broken down my cells were in my body. No one could help me. My spirit knew how sick my body was. It felt as though my body and spirit had separated from each other, - my spirit was watching how my physical body was suffering. For the first time in my life, I felt alone and helpless. Nothing and no-one could bring me healing in this desperate time, except God.

Throughout a child's life, parents are there to protect and nurture the child. Here, I was faced with a reality that not even my parents could help me. I knew the Lord was there, but I was too ill to speak, to pray, or even to think. My fate was in God's hands now.

***

Spring had started pushing through the last traces of cold weather, when I started getting better. Little did I know that my recovery would take the rest of the year, and that my whole life was about to change.

My diet had to be modified and my tennis training was kept to a minimum. The following year, revealed what a knock my body had taken from the former illness. I would only manage fifteen minutes of training, before wanting to collapse from utter exhaustion. My sugar levels and metabolism completely changed. For many years thereafter, I had to learn the delicate balance of food intake and activities. I found myself feeling miserable at times when my blood-sugar would plunge, especially during exercise periods.

After some consideration, I decided to leave professional tennis. There was no way my body would be able to perform the way it used to. There was no telling if I would ever fully recover from the effects of the jaundice.

It was a difficult time for me. Most of my identity was found in sports. I had no choice but to adjust, and find out what other purpose my life had. "*Do I search for a new dream? What else would interest me and bring me the same joy?*" I needed to find these answers as soon as my first year at university started.

To be honest, I was glad to be alive. Every day, health-wise was a challenge though. I appreciated the small things more. If things weren't done to perfection, I was fine with it. I had become more accepting of my limitations.

Other people in my position may have blamed God for having lost their dream, but I didn't see it that way. God was the One who helped me through the illness. He allowed this to happen for some reason. At the time I couldn't determine what that reason was.

The one thing that did tire me though, was not being able to feel normal and healthy on a daily basis. Mostly, it was a struggle to manage the unpredictability of my blood-sugar levels, - dealing with the different moods caused by it.

SECTION 2

Heaven

Psalm 16:11 ~ "...You will show me the way of life, granting me the joy of Your presence and the pleasures of living with You forever."

CHAPTER 4

Dying

What was happening?

Life is when you try to make the best of what you have been given. First year university was going to have to be my new start, a clean slate with a new destiny and path. New friends were being made and I was finding the studies quite fulfilling. I was even going to try out for the University Tennis Team.

My parents and I agreed that I'd be a day student and drive in for lectures, rather than staying at the university residence. I loved being home with my family. After all, my brother had done the same before me, and I saw the freedom he had. Health-wise my parents would be able to keep a closer eye on me, in case my blood-sugar levels acted up.

One night, while asleep at my parents' house, I didn't feel well at all. I had a sense of knowing in my spirit, that physically, something was wrong. If you have experienced serious illness before, you would be able to relate to what I am describing.

This particular night, for some unknown reason, I couldn't wake myself up. My heart was racing. Pressure was building up in my head. There was this ringing sound in my ears.

"Lord, what is happening? Lord, help me!" An utter desperation came over me. *"I think I'm dying and I cannot even scream for help! Why can't I wake up?"* I had never been so terrified in my life, - not even that time in the hospital, when I had the neck brace.

Suddenly there was this popping sensation. The pressure in my head had vanished. My heart wasn't racing any longer. In fact, my heart had stopped completely. The fear I experienced only seconds ago, had been instantly replaced by peace. When I was able to open my eyes, I looked around my room. I was standing at my bedside, staring at my lifeless body lying on the bed, peaceful.

"Am I dreaming?" From my point of view, the fragile body on the bed seemed very earthly and vulnerable.

It was still night-time. The house was quiet. Amazed at my body lying in bed, I noticed how light I felt, like a heavy burden had lifted off my shoulders. It was great! My physical body wasn't weighing me down any more. There was a feeling of immense peace, mingled with excitement.

> "I am the resurrection and the life. Anyone who believes in me will live, even after dying" (John 11:25 NLT).

> "... Those who die in the Lord will live, their bodies will rise again! ..." (Isaiah 26:19 NLT)

As you will recall, I give my heart to Christ at age sixteen, at a church camp. I believe that if I had not rededicated my life to the Lord that day, I wouldn't have had the heavenly experience I am about to share. Maybe I would have encountered hell instead.

> "... The dust will return to the earth, and the spirit will return to God who gave it" (Ecclesiastes 12:7 NLT).

In Ecclesiastes, it speaks about the spirit, soul and body. Your soul is your being, the essence of who you are, and who you know you are to be. It is the part that can think for its self. This is the part that has to accept Jesus Christ as its Lord and Saviour. The soul-part goes to heaven or to hell.

The body, which Ecclesiastes describes as the dust, is our physical bodies. When a person dies, the body perishes and is buried and left behind on earth.

The spirit is what God gives you when you are created. Once a person dies, the spirit-part returns to God. It is this very same spirit that God breathed into Adam, when he was created, which gave Adam's body life. The body cannot live without the spirit.

"Have I died? If I've died, it means I didn't pass out? I've been aware of everything. I haven't lost consciousness."

All these questions rushed through my mind as I stood in my bedroom in the dark.

"I still feel like myself. I still think normally, and haven't changed into someone that suddenly knows everything."

My total existence, of who Jeanne was, had not ended. I had thoughts and memories and ideas even though I had moved from one form into another.

> "... Look at My hands. Look at My feet. You can see that it's really Me" (Luke 24:39 NLT).

Luke 24 contains a section where Jesus appeared to His disciples after He had died and was raised from the dead. He was still Himself, – the same Jesus who died just a few days ago. He was moving into His glorified state. This was the same situation I found myself in.

As all these thoughts were coming up, I noticed that I started floating or moving away, upwards. I was able to move through the roof of our house and could see my neighbourhood. All was quiet. The street lights flickered, outlining the roads. I kept moving upward, into the heavens. As I looked up, I could see all the beautiful stars shining in the night sky. I didn't feel cold or afraid. Instead, I felt overwhelming peace and joy. An inexplicable happiness and love was upon me.

I had no control over the direction I was moving in. The feeling of freedom and lightness was so unexpected and welcoming. It was the strangest and most exciting experience yet.

> "... Yes, we are fully confident, and we would rather be away from these earthly bodies, for then we will be at home with the Lord" (2 Corinthians 5:8 NLT).

CHAPTER 5

The Stairs to Heaven

What would heaven seem like?

Travelling through the earth's atmosphere, I was now moving through some clouds. After a few moments I found myself standing at the bottom of a flight of stairs that appeared through the clouds.

"Where am I?" I carefully made my way up the steps. There were a couple of individuals randomly scattered around, on the stairs. Two of them sat close by, where I was passing. They were studying a book with a black cover. It wasn't the Bible, but I knew this book was all about God. *"Were these students studying subjects about God and heaven?"*

We recognize that the Bible consists of sixty-six books. We don't yet know and understand all of its content. It will take more than one person's life-time, to comprehend what the Bible teaches and reveals to us, - not to mention the multitude of layers of wisdom, locked up in each scripture. Now, imagine reading through these books found in heaven, containing the secrets of God, creation, His kingdom, the Holy Spirit, Christ Jesus, - and so I can continue! Our minds are constantly preoccupied with distractions and brokenness. Therefore, we can only cope with as much revelation as we find in the Bible currently.

Once I reached the top of the stairs, I saw the most beautiful university. The building was massive, unlike anything I'd ever seen. Its sheer size would have matched the enormity of the beautiful Louvre Museum in Paris. It was the colour of white-grey marble stone, majestic in nature. What a beautiful sight it was.

The university grounds were covered with short green grass, and elegant bricked pathways, winding through random tree placements. In the far distance I could see beautiful gardens and parks connected by similar stone walkways. It all looked so inviting. I decided to take a stroll along the walkways, and see where they would lead me. I still had no idea where I was, but I enjoyed exploring a new place anyhow.

The colours were amazing. The light itself was crisp and clear, as on a clear winter's day, without the cold of course. When I looked up into the soft blue sky, there was one very important object missing, - the sun. In all of the sky, I couldn't find the sun, and not a trace of any clouds. *"Where is the light coming from? And isn't it supposed to be night-time?"* Where I stayed it was still evening. This was too bizarre.

> "There shall be no night there: They need no lamp nor light of the sun, for the Lord God gives them light ..." (Revelation 22:5 NLT)

It was as though heaven was lit up by God's pure presence. Imagine, there was no sun, yet the whole place was filled with the purest light, which enhanced the colours of everything. The light seemed brighter, coming from a throne, which I noticed in the far distance. Since childhood, I've read about kingdoms and kings, but have never experienced their existence in my own lifetime. Sure, I have seen historic castles and palaces before, but nothing compared to this scenery!

> "... The city has no need of Sun or Moon, for the glory of God illuminated the city, and the Lamb is its light" (Revelation 21:23 NLT).

The gardens were neat and well-kept, as though special care was taken in cultivating every flower and blade of grass. The trees seemed to be evergreen. The plants and flowers appeared fresh and radiant, as though they had just blossomed. They couldn't bruise, or die.

There was something unique about the flowers though. They all appeared to be perfect, yet they were different. Some flowers seemed unusual, unlike any flowers I had seen before. Several were a combination of two or three flower-specimens, wrapped into one flower. For instance, there was a particular flower that seemed to be a combination of a rose and a carnation. Its red colour was so vivid and vibrant.

On earth, you are only able to enjoy a limited amount of possible creations. In heaven, expect much more variety and diversity. I would even be so bold as to say that everything on earth was inspired by heaven above. Everything on earth already exists in heaven. If your inspiration, ideas, and imagination, comes from God, then you are bound to create something out of this world. Heavenly ideas originating from heaven its self, with a limitless supply of ideas!

This would make sense, because God is the greatest creator, artist, and architect, ever to exist. The quality of all that God has created is displayed on earth, and in the universe, for all to see. Even more astounding to experience, is His quality of creativity in heaven. Like the diverse flowers, you will find things in heaven that do not exist on earth. God is limitless, and so too is His creation.

CHAPTER 6

People

People in heaven.

The gardens were amazing places of tranquillity. As I was walking through the gardens, I passed two strangers. It was an elderly couple, – even though they didn't seem old. They greeted and smiled. They looked familiar, yet I didn't know who they were. In my heart though, I sensed they knew God, which disqualified them as strangers. God was the common thread between all people. Here, in heaven, it appeared as though everyone knew each other.

The same is true of us here in our own lives. We are strangers until we get to know each other. In Genesis, it says that man is created in God's image, – which is true for each person. We all come from God, which makes us family, - whether you want to believe it or not.

Believers who have been Christians for a while will agree with the above statement. When you meet another Christian, there is this strange, familiar connection you share. This connection is instantly picked up in the spirit. It is a comfortable, pleasant, and inviting feeling. This connection is Jesus Christ, living inside of us.

In heaven, people are transformed into their most beautiful and perfect form, which is their glorified state. However, we are still able to recognize their appearance as it was on earth. When we remember people, we don't just remember their physical appearance, we also remember their character. A person's character forms part of the whole image of the person.

The plants that never die in heaven are actually in their glorified state. In the same way, our bodies in heaven are transformed into their divine and glorified state. Each living thing in heaven has its own specific glorified condition, bringing glory to God. One day, when we die, we will be changed and renewed, bringing glory to God.

> "Only dying bodies must be transformed into bodies that will never die; our mortal bodies must be transformed into immortal bodies" (1 Corinthians 15:53 NLT).

Of all the people I had encountered, I noticed that I never saw any of my friends or family there. One probable reason for this could have been that none of them had died at that time. Both my grandparents, from my mom and dad's side, were still alive. All my family members were still healthy and alive.

Suddenly, a very important question popped up. *"What do I do if none of them end up here with me? Are any of them saved?"* I did not know if any of them gave their hearts to Christ. It was never discussed before.

Even though my family was not there with me, I didn't quite miss them. It may seem insensitive and crazy, but let me explain what happens with a person in heaven. In heaven, you find yourself constantly in God's presence. His presence was everywhere. It would surround you and it would be inside of you, creating a sense of feeling complete, lacking nothing. There was no emptiness, sadness, or longing. The love of my family and friends had become completely part of me. Their love for me was fused with my spirit. I felt complete as all the love they had for me, was with me. I could never miss them. They were constantly part of me, as though they were right there with me.

When people die in our midst and we are left behind to continue living on without them, it seems like we have this empty space in our hearts. This is a true emptiness, because while they were alive, we gave them our love. When they die, they take this love with them. It doesn't belong to us anymore.

> "When the dead rise, they will neither marry or be given in marriage. In this respect they will be like the angels in heaven" (Matthew 22:30 NLT).

God's presence fulfils all our wants and desires. Marriage is no longer needed in heaven. We are a part of each person in heaven. Heaven gives the word "unity", a whole new meaning. People often speak about unity, but once they experience God's people in spiritual unity, they understanding completeness and strength on a different level. Imagine seeing different little candles, all light up, - which represent individual people. Now, imagine combining these candles to make one big fire. This flaming fire represents the unity of mankind under God. The brilliance and strength of this one fire, burns away darkness and evil.

> "There will be no more death or sorrow or crying or pain. All these things are gone forever" (Revelation 21:4 NLT).

The incredible love and peace I felt in heaven, was inexplicable. It was with me every second of every moment. To be a whole person in mind and spirit, for the first time, was an experience beyond words. There were no reminders of sorrow, pain, stress, anger, or anxiety. It was as though I was in love twenty-four hours a day, – constantly aware of all the good thoughts people had towards me. There was an awareness of all the beautiful actions and words spoken over me by others, in a period when I was still alive on earth. Even the things people said secretly, when I was not present in those conversations, became a part of me. All this was experienced, constantly, - forever.

The experience was overwhelming. God revealed the people who prayed for me, whether they were familiar people, strangers, or people I may not have expected prayer from. The Lord exposed people's beautiful thoughts towards me. He even showed me the most beautiful letters people wrote about me, which I never received. God revealed the gifts people kept and stored away, that I had given them through the years.

Every word, every thought, every letter and every gift I experienced, was from my passed life on earth, and from the people who remembered me long after my death. *"God, why didn't I realize how loved I was?"*

People don't share their true feelings of gratitude and thankfulness, while they are alive. If they do share it, they don't do it regularly enough. It seems easier for people to speak out in anger and disapproval. They find it easier to voice the negative and hurtful emotions, rather than the emotions of love and kindness.

The author, Rebecca Springer, once wrote in her book called, "Within Heaven's Gates", about the children who had died young, or at birth. She explained what happened to them in heaven. They are looked after by caregivers, and are watched over until their parents pass away on earth, and join them in heaven. It was so amazing to know that even if you had lost a baby or a child, you were already a parent. The children continued living in heaven, with their Father God, after they died.

The Lord then allowed me to experience the most amazing gift. In the same way people impacted my life, I saw how I impacted their lives. Every kindness I showed someone, any love I shared, the mercy I gave, and even the simple goodness I showed towards others while I was alive, came alive inside of me. The people's appreciation, gratitude, or thankfulness, became a part of me. Any kind of healing my words may have brought, became a part of me.

This is why I believe, that whatever we speak, or write about someone, even when they are not in our presence, or even when they are no longer alive, it all becomes a part of them for eternity.

If this is true about heaven, then the opposite must be true about hell? Imagine if you are not saved by Jesus Christ, and you mistreat people, bad-mouth them, cause them hurt; or bring destruction upon them. All your actions towards these people will become a part of you in hell. Whatever you have done to others will be done to you in hell, for eternity. What a terrible place to be. This is why the Lord wants to save all mankind, that they can escape eternal hell, and join Him in heaven forever.

CHAPTER 7

The Palace

Thousands of people at the palace.

The beautiful palace far in the distance, which caught my eye earlier, was engulfed in light. Alongside its walls were lines and lines of people, all in one queue. Maybe it was time for me to head in that direction. The thought crossed my mind that those people are probably gathering there to get a chance to appear before the King; to go before God to receive their judgement.

> "We must all stand before Christ to be judged. We will each receive whatever we deserve for the good or evil we have done in this earthly body" (2 Corinthians 5:10 NLT).

At this point I wasn't really sure what to do or where else to go.

"If I am dead, isn't that where I am supposed to be going?" It seemed like the most appropriate place to go at that time. As I thought this, I was there instantly! I couldn't believe it!

"How could this be, I didn't even have to walk all the way to get here?" At the speed of thought I was at the queue.

I noticed I could just think of being somewhere, and I would end up there without physically walking there. Whenever I wanted to pick something up, or do something physical, it was more my will that allowed it to happen, rather than my physical body doing it. In heaven, a person wasn't trapped by time, distance or space, because you were in your perfect state. Time had no relevance. Distance had no relevance. Space had no relevance.

Another way to explain this would be by looking at dreams. Think of how you experience your dreams. Your body is asleep, but while you dream, you are doing all these different things you would normally do while you were awake. It is very real to you. This is the closest explanation to how I experienced heaven.

Music and singing were constantly heard no matter where you went. Wherever I walked I heard worship. The most stunning music and the most beautiful voices just filled the air. It was in the atmosphere, – all around you. Imagine when you are walking in a shopping mall and you constantly hear music playing throughout the building. This was similar accept the entire heaven was filled with constant music.

I recall that when I came back to my life on earth, after my heavenly experience, the absence of continuous worship, and the presence of the Lord, was very difficult to adjust to. It was a terribly empty feeling. These days I will always have music on, in my car when I drive, at home, or wherever I can hear worship music.

Music, overall, is the closest thing on earth that can instantly bring me into God's presence. At times, it can even remind me of heaven the way I experienced it. Prayer and music are the links to heaven.

At the palace the music and singing was more audible and beautiful. The strong and soothing presence of the Lord brought a peace beyond words.

> "This great choir sang a wonderful new song in front of the throne of God" (Revelation 14:3 NLT).

There was an excitement in the depth of my spirit, – and to this day I still feel that anticipation in my stomach. It was the strangest thing. We all stood there, as though we were waiting for something incredible to happen.

As I observed this extremely long line of people, for some odd reason I didn't feel despondent in joining this queue. I wasn't thinking *"Oh no, this is going to take ages!"*

When I added myself to the back of the line, I felt calm and at peace. If I wanted to, I was even willing to stand there forever, waiting.

The overwhelming presence of not wanting to leave this place pulled people like a magnet. After some time, you would expect to feel bored, tired, irritated, or even frustrated, - but you don't. At times the line wasn't moving, and still you had peace.

Time didn't matter here. It was as though the day was progressing, at a leisurely pace. The sun would have been setting by now if I had to think in terms of earthly time, but night-time did not approach, and I wasn't even bothered by it.

Here in this place, you are not thinking about the past. You are not thinking about the future. You are living in this very moment. There are no worries about mundane things. There are no worries and stresses about serious things.

I wasn't afraid for my life being in danger. I wasn't afraid that someone was going to hurt or rob or kill me. There was no fear of being alone amongst the crowd of people. I wasn't concerned about where I was going to sleep, - if I ever needed it here -, and I was not concerned about food. There was no financial stress. There were no health worries. There was no fear at all. It was as though I knew in my heart that every need I had would be met forever.

CHAPTER 8

Heaven and Angels

If this was heaven?
And if those were angels?

The queue of people seemed endless, yet it was moving. The question started burning in my mind, "*Is this heaven? I need proof.*"

I went one step further in my thinking and wondered what would happen if I left my place in the queue, and moved right up to the front of the line, without asking anyone's permission.

"*This would be a good test surely, wouldn't it?*" The suggested thought felt so out of place, as though this type of thinking did not fit into the unseen stability of heaven. I instantly felt the conviction, but still decided to go through with this experiment of mine. Boldly, I walked right to the front of the line. There were two women talking to each other, but they didn't seem to notice me. No remarks were made about my attempted rudeness. They continued chatting as though I wasn't there.

The palace was beautiful and huge. The walls had a golden-white glow about them. At the entrance, two huge angels flanked the doorway. They didn't have any wings, but you could see they were of the palace guard. Most angels known to me would have wings, but I was aware that angels came in all sorts of shapes and sizes. These angels weren't armed. They just stood there with their arms folded. God's presence was so thick around the palace, that no external protection was needed from anything or anyone. These specific angels were dressed in white chiton, a type of garment, nothing extravagant, but still beautiful.

The remarkable characteristics of the angels are that they have no gender. They are beautiful angelic beings, with incredible peace, authority, and a sense of wisdom beyond our understanding. Remember, angels have existed since the dawn of creation, while we have only existed probably in a blink of an eye, – in God's time frame.

Angels are definitely holy creatures. They are not like humans. Angels are completely dedicated to the Word of God and only listen to His commands. Seeing them in this setting, surrounded by God's glory, His presence, and His splendour, gave me new insight into the Scripture that says, "You give Your angels charge". Believers take this phrase lightly, whereas the angels are completely committed to the Word of God.

An angel's entire existence is to please God alone, to serve Him, His children, and His kingdom. The angel is a servant with purpose and utter reverence for God. They live and portray the understanding of true worship towards the one and only almighty God. They depict this in all they do, in all they say, and in all their actions.

> "Angels are only servants – spirits sent to care for people who will inherit salvation" (Hebrews 1:14 NLT).

I noticed I got no reaction from the two ladies standing behind me. In front I saw the two angels who were guarding the entrance. *"What are they about to do to me?"* Thinking over my inquisitive actions, I realized it was more stupidity than bravery that got me into this situation. I was expecting a harsh rebuke or reprimand at any moment. There was even the expectation of being thrown out of the queue.

Nothing happened. Yet, a lot happened. The angel nearby me, turned its head and glanced at me with no expression on its face, arms still crossed over his chest. As the angel stared at me, I heard God speak to it.

"Leave her be, she's not supposed to be here."

Hearing God's command, the angel turned its head and continued patrolling the horizon with its eyes, as it did a moment ago. At that very instant I wanted the ground to swallow me up. Embarrassment was burning through my whole being! Thankfully, the angels and the people let me be. It seemed the angel recognised that I was no real threat to anyone. To the angel, I must have seemed more confused about my surroundings than anything else.

It only took me a couple of moments to rush back to the rear of the queue. With my head down, I promising myself not to look at anyone, let alone speak to anyone, that would tempt me to get myself into more trouble. I also felt ashamed at testing God. It was pretty clear to me then, that I had died, and I was in heaven.

Having had a lot of time to think about my ridiculous behaviour, it became clear how God's laws made up the very existence of heaven. This law was not written somewhere on a scroll, for all to see. It existed inside of us, and in the very fabric of heaven.

None of our negative, selfish, destructive actions are allowed in heaven. It cannot exist here. It is like oil and water that can never mix. On earth, we live in a fallen world. We, as human beings have this mixture of good and evil living inside of us – the spirit of God and the fallen nature of man. In heaven they are completely separate. That is why God's Word says we need to be a holy people.

God's moral fibre is woven into the fabric of heaven, and into all creation. This is why God also needs to be woven into us, into our souls, and into our spirits. This is made possible through His Son, Jesus Christ, and the power of the Holy Spirit.

In heaven, learning and revelation happens very quickly. Your mind is fresh and crystal clear. Distractions have no power to infiltrate your mind. When you learn something, it's permanent and remains forever. It is unlike here on earth, where your body gets drained, your mind gets exhausted and wonders, you day dream, or you struggle to grasp the concepts. In heaven you have complete understanding and complete recollection, - a supernatural clarity.

> "Now we see things imperfectly, like puzzling reflections in a mirror, but then we will see everything with perfect clarity. All that I know now is partial and incomplete, but then I will know everything completely, just as God now knows me completely" (1 Corinthians 13:12 NLT).

CHAPTER 9

Understanding Life

Presenting our lives before God.

An Indian lady, about my age, was standing before me, in the queue. She turned to me and started up a conversation. At first, I was a little sceptical and didn't talk much. I mostly listened to her conversation. As she was chatting, I noticed her baby son in her arms. She was very kind and pleasant. After some time into the discussion, I realized that I actually knew her from my previous life. We seemed to be friends, even though we have never formally met, prior to this moment. Why did I only recognize her now? What was familiar about her? What had changed in our conversation that led me to believe I know her?

While we were bonding, the queue had progressed until we found ourselves in the front. Once again, the two angels from my earlier encounter flanked the doorway. When I glanced back at the line of people, I noticed that everyone was carrying something in their hands; - small packages. I was the only one not carrying anything.

The packets contained an accumulation of all the events that happened in their lives, - memories, thoughts, motives and actions, – both good and bad. Each person was to present their packet, signifying their life, to God.

I realized I didn't have anything to present. *"Was I unprepared? It's not like anybody told me to come with something?"* Even if I was told about the package, I don't think I would have known what to choose that would symbolize my life. I decided to present myself as the package. My own life, my own being, would have to be laid down before God, as a representation of my life.

When I saw each person's life-pack, if I could call it such, I wondered, *"Would my life be good enough to bring before the Lord? Were there things I would be ashamed of? Would there be things God would be proud of or disappointed in? Will He show me His disappointment? Will I see what impact I made on other people?"* Then the question came up: *"Am I ready to face the truth about my life and all the decisions I had made?"*

Listen well to what I am saying at this moment. Read this slowly and take to heart what I am about to share. Do not fool yourself with excuses and blame-shifting. Your life, your actions, and your decisions, have all been your choice. No matter what troubles you have faced, and no matter what people and life may have done to you, your choice to live righteously, to live with joy, and to live with forgiveness, is still your decision.

Our allowance to entertain selfishness, stubbornness, and un-forgiveness, leads to the hardening of our hearts. Hurt and anger fuel our reason for building the wrong walls around ourselves. All these walls end up shutting God out of our hearts. Yes, some may say they love God, but when it comes to loving people, they cringe. Some may feel that people are not worthy of their love any longer, - especially when it involves hurt. That kind of thinking is caused by believing the lie of the devil.

When we cannot love people or ourselves, we cannot love God. We then only show conditional love, while God has called us to love unconditionally. Would you like to only be loved conditionally? No, of course not. You would like to be loved unconditionally.

Some may feel God has let them down in life, or even believe He abandoned them. They will confess that they do not love God any longer. The anger they carry with them, automatically hinders their ability to receive love, and to give love. After some time, they find themselves in this circle of emptiness, and loneliness. Remember, the devil is out there to separate humanity from the love of God. The enemy will use lies and deceit against us to succeed.

How well do you know God? Have you tried to get to know Him? If you truly seek Him and get to know Him, then you will start having a real heart-to-heart conversation with Him. You may even get the answers you have been seeking. Don't expect the right answers from people who also don't know God. Go to God personally. Job did, because he had a relationship with God.

> "But if from there you seek the Lord your God, you will find him if you look for him with all your heart and with all your soul" (Deuteronomy 4:29 NIV).

Our relationship with God is connected to our lives, and how we live it. One day, we will present it all to Him. In love, He will look at our "life-packs", and observe each item. These items will be our spoken words, our thoughts, our motives, our actions, our relationships with God and man, living life with excellence, our focus in life, our decision-making, and our dreams.

In Part II we will look at what the Lord reveals about these items.

CHAPTER 10

The Throne Room of God

The splendour of the King.

My new found friend and I were standing in the queue at God's palace, awaiting her turn to enter the throne room. When it was time, my friend made her way through the door with her baby.

As I watched her walk across this huge foyer towards the throne room, my eyes fell on the velvet red carpet, inter-woven with small pieces of gold. The room was surrounded by towering golden palace walls. It was beautiful and spacious.

> Then as I looked, I saw a door standing open in heaven, and the same voice I had heard before spoke to me like a trumpet blast. The voice said, "Come up here, and I will show you what must happen after this". And instantly I was in the Spirit, and I saw a throne in heaven and someone sitting on it. The one sitting on the throne was as brilliant as gemstones – like jasper and carnelian. And the glow of an emerald circled His throne like a rainbow ... (Revelation 4:1-4 NLT)

I saw God's throne. It was beautiful and brilliant. He was surrounded by golden white light as He sat on the throne. I dared not look up towards His face, as I was afraid I might die. The place was filled with His glory and brilliance, which lit up the throne room, the palace and heaven itself. What I could make out were His legs and feet, so beautiful and powerful.

Many people were visible before God's throne. I sensed in my Spirit, that this almighty God of ours knew I was there in His midst. His thoughts were aware of me, but His attention was upon those He addressed in front of His exquisite throne. This was the most insignificant I had ever felt in my whole existence. I didn't mind it, because I didn't know how I would have reacted if God's full attention was suddenly turned towards me?

"Was I nervous? ", you may ask. Most definitely!! I didn't know what to expect. *"What do I say when I go before God? Will I have any words to describe this feeling in my heart?"* At that moment, I was in the throne room of a magnificent God; the God I heard about in Sunday school; the God I read about in the Bible; the God I had a relationship with while alive on earth. I had no words worth speaking… My mouth wouldn't move… I couldn't form any useful words … No words existed to describe this truth, this reality of almighty God. I felt like Isaiah in the Bible, where He said the following:

> "'Woe to me!' I cried. 'I am ruined! For I am a man of unclean lips, and I live among a people of unclean lips, and my eyes have seen the King, the Lord Almighty.' "(Isaiah 6:5 NIV)

Everything I had read about God was true! This was it. My life was in fact over. I had died and I am in heaven now. It was all true! And in a couple of moments I was about to enter the throne room of almighty God and present my life to Him…

"Why do I feel so unprepared?" To be honest, nothing can prepare you for meeting 'The God of all Creation', who thought of you before time

itself. When the truth is manifested as God almighty, sitting before you, waiting for you to present yourself before His throne, all you had ever known or thought you had ever known, crumbles to nothing.

You cannot help but be instantly humbled, and instantly enthralled by His majesty, power, glory, beauty, authority, and endless love. In an instant, you understand the awe, and true reverential fear all the angels in heaven display towards this King of Kings.

> "The Lord has established his throne in heaven, and his kingdom rules over all. Praise the Lord, you his angels, you mighty ones who do his bidding, who obey his word. Praise the Lord, all his heavenly hosts, you his servants who do his will" (Psalm 103:19-21 NIV).

The overwhelming power of God, stirs a respectful fear in humanity. Yet, this fear is simultaneously overwhelmed by His unconditional love for us. Now, I comprehend the fear the enemy and his demons must possess towards God. Concurrently, I understand His great love and goodness towards His children, all because of Jesus Christ, His precious Son.

> "I tell you, my friend, do not be afraid of those who kill the body, and after that can do no more. But I will show you whom you should fear: Fear him who, after the killing of the body, has power to throw you into hell. Yes, I tell you, fear him" (Luke 12:4-5 NKJV).

God is all-powerful, and Satan, with all his principalities, are rendered powerless in the presence of God and His light. The name of Jesus is so mighty, that by the mention of His name, the enemy flees, running away from the light and truth. The children of God will forever be covered by God's love, grace and justice. A believer is saved by grace, through Jesus. His never-ending love for His children provides security, protection, and safety.

Children, who love their mom or dad, know that they will be disciplined by their parents when they have done wrong. However, they know their parents still love them. God is the same with us. Just like children have respect for their parents, we should have the same admiration for God.

The thought never crossed my mind, that one day I would have to describe God. Then again, I had never imagined I would appear in His manifested presence in such a real way such as this. I still battle to verbalize the encounter. I had reached the end of myself and found God there, in all His splendour and majesty…

CHAPTER 11

Time

Observing my life from start to finish.

My friend was walking across to the throne room, when I noticed her having dropped one of her memories. Suddenly, a surge of worry overwhelmed me. I felt troubled. I knew she had to have all her memories of her life-events with her, to present before God. Without thinking, I hurried into the foyer to pick up the item she had dropped. I tried calling her back, but she continued into the throne room.

When I approached the object located on the carpet, I noticed it was a wrist watch. *"What a strange item?"* Not quite what I had expected. As I picked it up, I realized the watch was mine! How can this be? She was carrying an item that belonged to me?

Staring into the face of the watch, I saw it contained all **my** life recollections. In a couple of seconds, I saw my entire life play out before me, - from the day I was born until the day I died. The realization of what I was holding in my hand was too overwhelming. My friend had dropped this part of her memories, because this watch included the memories we would have shared together as friends, had I not died. We were still destined to meet and become friends. While I was here in heaven, it meant I had died before we had an opportunity to meet.

She didn't have anything to present to God regarding her relationship with me.

My friend had no choices, words, actions, or motives, tied to me. She didn't need to present any of this to the Lord, because it never happened. If I didn't return to my life, I would change her life, my life, and many others.

There is no time in heaven, except this very moment; the "now". Time needn't exist in heaven. A person can use the example of looking at a pen.

When you look at it, you see the whole pen. You see the beginning of the pen and you see the end of the pen, - all at once. God sees our lives in the exact same way. He sees our beginning part, middle part, and end part all at once. Thankfully, nothing surprises Him, while we can only live our lives in one direction. We can only live from the beginning of life to the end. In this life journey, we are experiencing and living in the present.

God showed me my life from His perspective; resulting in me seeing my whole life at once. Time, is only relevant in our lives on earth. We live forward. We cannot go back and we cannot live in the future. God is present in every period of our lives. He is present in our past, our present, and our future. We live in the present – the now, which is separated by a yesterday and a tomorrow (or earlier today, and later today). We are actually only alive in this very moment. This is why I saw my friend there. She was still alive on earth, but in heaven there is no time. God was trying to show me something important – that He was even in control of time.

The realization emerged of what a huge impact we make on the lives of other people. I saw how responsible I was for my actions towards other people. Whether I was present in their lives, or absent from it, it made a huge difference.

The time we are given on earth, can be spent as abundant as possible; or wasted, or ended forcibly. It is our choice. Many questions arise when suicide is discussed in society. Personally I have lost friends to suicide, and those funerals are usually the hardest to attend. Some of them were friends who were not born again, and others were born again. Depression and pain affects both Christians and non-Christians. Suicide is a spirit that needs to be eradicated as soon as it is recognized in someone's life. When the enemy cannot overcome us physically, he will turn to attacking a person's mind, to turn the person against themselves.

I had seen God's mercy go beyond our understanding, especially when it comes to suicide. When you have accepted the Lord Jesus Christ into your heart, and are born again, but later in life face adversity which may lead to you taking your own life, there will be forgiveness for it. Sin is sin.

Hear me carefully regarding this matter. If you are saved and do die because of suicide, yes, you will be with the Lord in heaven, but the Lord will reveal to you what you had taken from your own life, and from the lives of others. You did not only steal from these people's lives, but you have stolen from God. You have stolen the time that God had given you to live out your purpose – the very reason He created you, and gave you life on earth.

When we lose people to suicide, we mourn the following facts:

- We were not given enough time to experience them.
- They were not given enough time to experience us.
- We cannot be blessed by what they carried inside of them.
- They cannot be blessed by what we could have offered them.
- We cannot experience their gifting and talents.
- We lose out on their personality, their character, their ideas and their influence.
- We miss out on forgiveness, on love, on friendship, on joy, on laughter, on success, and on sharing life with them.

- We will never get to see the person live out their destiny and purpose.
- We will miss spending time with them, speaking to them, crying with them, growing with them.

If you ever reach the place where you want to give up and quit living, turn back to this chapter and read it. You are too precious to God and His wonderful plan for your life. You are too precious to the people in your life, and to the people you are to still meet.

Speak to someone you can trust, when you hit a low. Find encouragement and love from those around you. If there are none of these people, cry out to God to touch you. Ask Him to send you loving and beautiful friends who will care about you

When Jesus was in the garden of Gethsemane, He was praying intensely to God. There was a battle in His spirit and mind. The human side of Jesus must have been afraid of dying. His closest disciples even disappointed Him, by falling asleep instead of praying with Him. As Jesus was praying to God the Father, He sent Jesus an angel to be with Him that night.

> "'Father, if you are willing, take this cup from me; yet not my will but yours be done.' An angel from heaven appeared to him and strengthened him" (Luke 22:42-43 NIV).

If you feel no one understands you, and you are all alone in whatever you are facing, know that Jesus is praying for you in heaven. Cry out to Him. He will hear you and send help. Receive His love for you.

To tie up my experience regarding time, and this friend I met in heaven, I will share some future events that related to this. After I had returned to my life, only two years later, when I was a third year student at University, I met this lady whom I spoke to in heaven. In our third year together, she had fallen pregnant with a boy – the same boy I saw her carry in her arms in heaven. Isn't God absolutely amazing? This had to happen in such a way, that I would know that what I had experienced was very real.

CHAPTER 12

Jesus

The tree of life and the river of life.

After seeing my entire life in the face of this wrist watch, I felt my Spirit being pulled away to another place. Moments passed, when I found myself standing next to the Lord Jesus, under a huge tree planted on a river bank. The tree's branches stretched out to the sides in full splendour. This was the tree of life. It was so peaceful here. The waters created a sound of peace and life. This was the river of life. The scene was amazingly beautiful and tranquil.

The Lord was dressed in a casual white robe, and wore beautiful sandals. He was quite relaxed, and it seemed as though He had been waiting there for me a short while. He greeted me with a loving smile.

> "On each side of the river of living water stood the tree of life ..." (Revelation 22:2 NIV)

When sharing this part of my testimony with people, most of them, especially children, always want to hear about how Jesus appeared. Their eyes would light up with excitement as I share with them. After I would describe how I saw Jesus in heaven, I would make a point of including this simple truth; - the Lord's incredible love for us, is very overpowering. Our physical bodies are not able to contain its vibrancy.

Our simple minds cannot comprehend it. The Lord approaches us very gently. He will never cast fear on us, or embarrass us. The Lord is patient and understands where we are, on an emotional and spiritual level.

Most people, who have encountered the Lord, would describe it as follows. He would approach a person in a way that would feel most comfortable for them; and meet with them at a location they best identified with Him.

Many people have written books about their encounters with the Lord Jesus. Personally, I have friends who have had significant encounters with Him too. To each of them He appeared in an individual way, that wasn't threatening to them, but safe and familiar.

When you read about people's different encounters with Jesus Christ, after His resurrection, it resonates with the fact I have just shared. In John 20, for instance, Jesus was encountered as a gardener.

> "At this, she turned around and saw Jesus standing there, but she did not realize that it was Jesus. 'Woman', he said, 'why are you crying? Who is it you are looking for?' Thinking he was the gardener, she said ..." (John 20:14-16 NKJV)

The Lord only revealed Himself, once the person was ready to see Him. Some, while travelling on the road, encountered Him as a travelling stranger, and didn't take much notice of Him.

> Now behold, two of them were travelling that same day to a village called Emmaus, which was seven miles from Jerusalem. And they talked together of all these things which had happened. So it was, while they conversed and reasoned, that Jesus Himself drew near and went with them. But their eyes were restrained, so that they did not know Him. And He said to them, 'What kind

> of conversation is this that you have with one another as you walk and are sad?' (Luke 24:13-17 NKJV)

Jesus faced me and started talking with me. He spoke about my previous life, up until my death, including all the events that had happened to me. After discussing my past, He indicated that I was about to see my future on earth, if I decided to return to my life there.

> "God can point to us in all future ages as examples of the incredible wealth of His grace and kindness towards us, as shown in all He has done for us who are united with Christ Jesus" (Ephesians 2:7 NIV).

As I watched the future events of my life unfold, I noticed how completely different it would be, to the life I had previously. My future held the prospect of peace, happiness, and a good life. This was not the current picture of my life. There were wonderful people I would meet, genuine people who would love me and care about me. I was going to minister, have a healing ministry, and pray for a lot of people. I was going to travel to many places and still do many things.

It was hard to believe this could be my life. Before I died, I was struck with illness. My professional sporting career had come to an end. It seemed as though my life had ended, but what Jesus revealed was a completely turned around life. I would be heading in another direction. It was beautiful, peaceful, and filled with opportunities for real joy, - even in challenging moments.

Jesus assured me, that once my life was lived and over, I would come home to meeting Him in that very same spot, under the tree, next to the river.

The Lord made one thing very clear. In order for me to have a blessed future, I couldn't continue the way I was living. Real change had to come. It would be essential for me to lay down my own will, my selfish plans, and be obedient to His purpose for my life. I had to surrender my life completely to Him.

As the Lord explained this, I felt a wall rise up in my heart. *"Give up the things I want most in my life? I can't do that. I've lost so much already! What else am I suppose to give up?"* I think Jesus saw the internal struggle I had. The Lord recognized the disappointment I had in knowing that He might be asking too much of me, something I wasn't able to do.

'And what if I don't change?' I asked, with the hope of not having to change who I am.

The Lord looked at me, and then came up really close to me. Gently He explained that if change did not come, my future life would become miserable, and even unbearable, - worse than what it was. A sinking feeling welled up inside of me.

"I can't do this," I realized.

'Even if I wanted to change Lord, I don't know how? I have tried, but nothing has worked. It has been so hard for me, and now you are asking the very thing that seems impossible for me to do?'

I was angry with the Lord. I felt He was cruel to have shown me a great life that lay ahead, but then expecting the impossible from me, before I can claim it. My heart was aching. There was a sorrow in me I couldn't contain, – a despair I didn't want to recognize. It felt as though I was left with no choice.

'Then, I choose not to go back to my life, Lord. Let me stay here. I don't want to go back. I cannot change what you have asked me to change. So I guess I'll never have the life You promised.' The Lord was holding me and said the following, **'Yes, I know you can't change these things, but if you allow me, I will change them for you.'**

With those words, the real question came up in my heart, "D*o I want Jesus to change me?"* That choice would be mine to make. *"Do I want Him to change the things I thought made me happy?"* Were the things I pursued ever really true happiness, or were they counterfeit? If so, then it meant I had spent my entire life pursuing the wrong things that I thought would bring contentment.

This new reality was becoming too heavy for me to reflect on. Instead of experiencing Jesus with a glad heart, it was replaced with a sense of heaviness. I didn't want to go back to my life anymore. Here, in heaven, I was complete, – lacking nothing. The Lord somehow removed the heaviness in my heart. I felt it fade away like a distant memory that wouldn't upset me any longer.

We all face aspects in our lives that bring about challenges, habits, temptations, fears, worries, situations, or things we cannot change. We may have tried to bring about change though our own will-power, but we keep failing, not moving forward, not finding victory over the things we struggle with.

What Jesus was saying, is that I had to choose to allow Christ to change the things I couldn't change. The Lord has greater things in store for our lives. Most of the time, we end up getting in the way of our own blessings. We become our own worst enemy.

I want to encourage you, whether you have done time in prison, have a reputation to lie, steal, abuse substances, gambling issues, struggling with lust, any sexual perversions; or thoughts; only the Lord can set you truly free from it. No one else can, - not even you. Once you have decided to honestly turn away from the things that are destroying your life, the Lord Jesus Christ will come and help you overcome them.

> "Yes, I am the vine; you are the branches. Those who remain in Me, and I in them, will produce much fruit. For apart from Me you can do nothing" (John 15:5 NLT).

All you need to do is tell the Lord you really want change and He will do it for you. He will guide, teach, and lead you as you work through your challenges. He will send the right people who can walk a road with you. He will guide you and point you in the right direction.

The Holy Spirit is the secret power behind setting people free. One very important note I need to make here, is about the infilling of the Holy Spirit. When you decide to take on your challenges, remember that the Holy Spirit will equip and strengthen you, making all of this possible. Being baptized in the Holy Spirit is one of the most powerful experiences you can ever have. It will help manifest the change in your life. The Holy Spirit makes it possible, by putting the word of God into action. I got baptized with the Holy Spirit while I was in heaven. I was saturated by Him, because He is in the very atmosphere of heaven.

> But the Comforter (Counsellor, Helper, Intercessor, Advocate, Strengthener, Standby), the Holy Spirit, whom the Father will send in My Name [in My place, to represent Me and act on My behalf], He will teach you all things. And He will cause you to recall (will remind you of, bring to remembrance) everything I have told you. (John 14:26 AMP)

Be honest with yourself when you decide to do this. Don't fool yourself, or even try fooling God, by saying you want to change, but deep in your heart you're not ready. You need to want to walk away from the old things, and walk into the direction of the new. Keep in mind that there will be no turning back to the old. Once your mind is made up, it is done.

You need to be a hundred percent committed and dedicated. God is going to be a hundred percent committed to this too! Trust Him constantly. This will be the greatest challenge of your life. This challenge will last until the day you become perfect in God's presence.

You may ask, 'What do I get in return for this change?' You will receiver complete freedom for your soul, including having peace beyond measure. And everyone who sees you flourish in every area of life will want what you have!

CHAPTER 13

Leaving Heaven

Not quite the end.

After my encounter with Jesus, I suddenly found myself back in the palace foyer, lying on the beautiful red and gold carpet. I was overcome with heaviness. I couldn't get up. My spirit felt lead-heavy. *"What was happening to me? Have I been spiritually overwhelmed by what Jesus has revealed to me?"* I needed help, as I couldn't move or speak. It felt as though I was pushed into the palace floor.

Instantly, four angels appeared by my side. They pick me up, one for each arm and leg. These angels were enormous, with glorious wings. They were extremely powerful, yet gentle with me. They lifted me up and took me back to the grand stair-case where I had first entered heaven. I could see the earth below. It was still night-time. I wondered how many days had passed since I arrived here. Or was this still the same evening I left home?

The angel that held my one arm had crystal clear blue eyes. "You must go back," the angel explained. It wasn't a command, but more a request. The angel wanted me to make the choice between remaining here in heaven, or return to my life on earth. I didn't want to go back. For me, there was no reason to go back. It may sound insensitive, but here, with

God, I was happy, loved and healed, - I was complete. I didn't miss my family or my friends, as they were part of my spirit constantly.

While I was deciding on what to do, a scripture came to mind, where God's word said that we need to obey God's messengers. In this very moment, I had an angel of the Lord speaking to me. I didn't want to disobey the angel, so I said, "Okay". Instantly, in the spirit, my hands release the hands of the angels. Then as I started descending back to earth, I remembered all I experienced in heaven.

"What am I doing?" I panicked. Who would give up heaven to go back to a life of pain, suffering and death? I tried grasping the angel's arms, but my hands went right through its arms. There was no turning back, - I had made my decision.

> How you are fallen from heaven, O Day Star, son of Dawn! How you are cut down to the ground, you who laid the nations low! You said in your heart, 'I will ascend to heaven; above the stars of God I will set my throne on high; I will sit on the mount of assembly in the far reaches of the north; I will ascend above the heights of the clouds; I will make myself like the Most High'. But you are brought down to Sheol, the far reaches of the pit. (Isaiah 14:12-15 ESV)
>
> "And he said to them, 'I saw Satan fall like lightning from heaven.'" (Luke 10:18 ESV)

When you make a decision in heaven, it is made. You cannot go back on it. Jesus said in Luke 10, how He saw Satan (the Day Star in Isaiah 14) and his fellow angels, fall to earth. God had banished them from heaven. When the angels made their own decision in whom to follow and serve, they could not go back on their decision.

In heaven, your word is your word, and you are bound by it. Whether that word is good or bad, once it is spoken, it is given life and power. On earth, at times, we are thoughtless concerning the words we speak. We go back on our word. We compromise. We don't honour what we promise. We find it easy to break our word, since we don't see the direct implications of it. We may think we get away with not honouring our word, but we don't get away with it. It just takes longer for the repercussions of our actions to become evident.

Here are some examples of typical repercussions:

- Wounding the expectations or hopes of other people.
- Breaking people's trust, which was build up over time.
- Disappointing friends or family by careless behaviour.
- Becoming unreliable.
- Each time we go back on our word, our conscience becomes numb.
- Our promises become empty and meaningless.
- Our words to others lose its power.

We don't like it if someone goes back on their word towards us, so why do we do it to others? We take it so lightly when changing our minds about decisions. Many people don't think their decisions through before making them. This will not do in heaven. It will not be tolerated or allowed, because it is not the personality of God. God almighty never goes back on His word. He even says in Bible that we need to remind Him of the promises He has made to us.

> "I have set watchmen upon your walls, O Jerusalem, who will never hold their peace day or night; you who [are His servants and by your prayers] put the Lord in remembrance [of His promises], keep not silence," (Isaiah 62:6 AMP)

Let our yes be yes, and our no be no. Once you have spoken your word, follow it through and act on it. If your actions are not in line with your words, God cannot trust you to be used in people's lives. People themselves won't even trust you.

As I continued to descent away from heaven, ever closer to the earth, I saw it covered in darkness, with lights in the areas of civilization. It took only moments before I saw my country, then my area, followed by my house. Moments after that, I was back in my room. It was still dark. No one had woken up yet. Nobody noticed that I had been gone. My body lay so still on the bed. In comparison to our beautiful spirit bodies, or spirit-man, I realized how fallen and fragile our earthly bodies seemed. Our spirit is perfect in every way.

Our spirit is more glorious than our bodies. Our bodies are in a fallen world where it ages and deteriorates. There is no deterioration in heaven. This is why your body is transformed into its perfect state. God's presence alone regenerates all life and is life-sustaining. In heaven, you are constantly aware of God's manifestation. Here on earth, we tend to move away from the presence, be it because of our actions, state of mind, or places we find ourselves in.

> "When Moses came down from Mount Sinai with the two tablets of the covenant law in his hands, he was not aware that his face was radiant because he had spoken with the Lord" (Exodus 34:29 NIV).

When Moses was on Mount Sinai, he was constantly in God's presence. His face was radiant, and his physical body remained strong and healthy.

Without effort, I slipped back into my earthly, lifeless body. It was so heavy. Suddenly, I felt confined. Instantly, I heard myself gasp for air. Immediately pain flooded my body. I became aware that I was in pain. I felt confused and afraid. I forced my eyes to open and wake up. I was sore and tired all over. Lack of oxygen caused pins and needles in my arms. It was a struggle to sit up. My arms felt heavy.

"Was all this just a dream?" I tried getting up to go to the bathroom and rinse my face. My legs were so earth-bound. Once in the bathroom, I let the water run, splashing my face. My brain felt slow, but yet I remembered everything that had just happened.

My spirit wasn't free anymore, but restricted to this space, time and body. The sense of peace and completeness had left me. Gazing at myself in the mirror, disappointment crept into my heart. I'm alive and back in *the land of the living*, so to speak. *"Lord will I be okay? Who will I tell about this experience? Will they believe me?"*

SECTION 3

The Start of My Life

"To have a second chance means you have an opportunity to do things better."

CHAPTER 14

Adjusting

A longing to return to heaven.

Months and even years after this incredible experience, I was facing trying times. Adjusting to the absence of heaven was tough. I was struggling with the change. To know what heaven was like, and have that reality taken from you, was like experiencing love by your husband or wife in marriage, and then losing them to death, shortly after you got married. The finality of loss, separation, sorrow, and depression was hard to accept. To feel so separated from God is unbearable. No one would be able to understand, what was revealed and what was lost that night.

Years on end, I would wake up in the mornings, expecting to wake up in heaven. With all my heart, I wanted to go back. I'd find myself praying each night, before bedtime, that the Lord would come fetch me while I sleep. Every morning I would wake up though, still in the same place.

> "I'm torn between two desires: I long to go and be with Christ, which would be far better for me" (Philippians 1:23 NLT).

Honestly, I had realized I was not ready for heaven. My thinking needed to change. Regardless of many short-comings, the Lord would have allowed me to stay in heaven, if I chose it. He loved me enough to not have forced this decision on me.

The music in heaven had a tremendous influence on me. I found myself missing it the most, as it elevated and enhanced the presence of God. Worship instantly brings me into the manifestation of the Lord. It is the only time I feel like I'm back in heaven again.

Every day, since then, I would compare my actions. Would they measure up to heavenly standards? Daily, I would wonder if my actions and thoughts had matured enough to be of a holy nature, as it is in heaven. At the end of the day, I had to make peace with the fact that I'm not going back to heaven soon. I had to make peace with my life as I was at that moment. There was nothing I could do to change this. Facing a world filled with hurt, pain, suffering, selfishness, sickness, corruption, hatred, murder, tiredness, etc., was daunting for me. I found myself separated from heaven, – separated from wholeness, love, completeness, everlasting peace, everlasting strength, revitalization, hearing worship everywhere and every day, freshness of mind, and contentment.

I spent hours in prayer, asking the Lord, *"How do I cope? How do I live without the constant manifestation of God?"* It was not easy. The enemy knew what I had experienced, and tried really hard to discourage me. Many years later, the Lord led me to the scripture, Psalm 16:11, which provided the encouragement I needed throughout my life. It became my personal life scripture:

> "... You will show me the way of life, granting me the joy of Your presence and the pleasures of living with You forever." (Psalm 16:11 NLT)

Like the flowers that were infused with one another in heaven, the Lord was about to infuse Himself with me. It will not be of my own doing, but by His power. Through His Holy Spirit, we would become inseparable.

> "Yes, I am the vine; you are the branches. Those who remain in Me, and I in them, will produce much fruit. For apart from Me you can do nothing" (John 15:5 (NLT).

Furthermore, the blessing, honour, and grace that comes from God, will provide all that I need for the years to come. It will renew my strength to honour His name every day. There will be nothing to fear, because He will be here with me, to comfort and protect me.

My prayer for you this day is that you will become infused with the Lord, through His Holy Spirit. May your life be blessed, honoured and filled with grace, no matter what your circumstances. May you wake up every day and not fear; knowing that each need will be met by the Lord; and that He will always bring comfort and protection to you and your family.

Even though I miss heaven, a remnant was left behind in my spirit. This touch of heaven caused a permanent change in my soul, spirit and body. One cannot help but expect a tangible transformation, when one has encountered heaven and God in such a way:

- I was able to pray in tongues. (Due to the Holy Spirit being the presence of God in heaven)
- I was able to play the piano more freely under the leading of the Holy Spirit.
- Even my art and drawings changed, because I had changed! Artists know that their art work changes when they change spiritually.
- After my water baptism in church, I was completely healed health-wise. The Lord had balanced out every area of my physical body.
- I have met the most amazing people in my life. Mighty people of God.
- The Lord has started healing and restoring my family.

CHAPTER 15

As It Is In Heaven

Learning how to live on earth as it is in heaven.

The world and society, has its own view on how we should live our lives, but heaven seemed very different to life in the world. The two realms seemed light-years apart from each other. That is when the Lord answered my question I posed in an earlier chapter, *"Lord, am I going to be okay?"*

The revelation was that we can experience heaven, in our own lives here on earth. Peace, wholeness, acceptance, and love, all originate from the Lord Jesus Christ. To have this, we need to search for Him, and work at discovering Him. We don't need to wait until we enter heaven to be with the Father. God wants us to have this heavenly life (Kingdom life) here and now, but we can only receive it through Christ Jesus. Perhaps, this heavenly story needed to be told, for other people to hear there is true life in the midst of a broken world. When you are outside of God's love, you will find this very hard to understand. Something happens within your spirit when you are found in the love of Jesus Christ. This transforming power belongs to the Trinity (God the Father, God the Son, and God the Holy Spirit) alone. There is no other that has this power.

Over time, I got to know God's grace in my life, the freedom to get up and try again, especially when I got it wrong. At times, it is hard to do what God asks of us. However, take comfort in the scripture, Philippians 2:6-8, where Jesus laid down His power as a King, and took on the humble life of a servant. Jesus had to lay down His own will, for that of the Father. In the same way, we have to lay down our lives to the will of the Father. It is all about Him, – about God. It is not about us. Yet we get blessed by experiencing the glory of Jesus Christ inside of us.

> Though He was God, He did not think of equality with God as something to cling to. Instead, He gave up His divine privileges; He took the humble position of a slave and was born as a human being. When He appeared in human form, He humbled Himself in obedience to God and died a criminal's death on the cross. (Philippians 2:6-8 NIV)

The Lord Jesus faced the same struggles we face today. He understands our daily challenges, but He has the power to help us overcome them. Jesus had the same power to overcome His own trials.

The desire in my heart grew, to start becoming the person I wanted to be in heaven, – to become a Kingdom citizen here on earth. I wanted to mirror God's Kingdom, His character. There was a yearning to start living like someone who came from heaven. Then I would know God's very laws would function fully in my heart. I wanted to reflect what I had experienced in heaven, to the world around me, which also meant reflecting God's nature. At some stage I even wanted the Lord to rather return and take my place, because I realized my constant failure. Perfection is not the point. Despite our imperfections and failures, He is still able to use us, and change us. The Lord wants us to only declare His love to others, because this knowledge that they are loved despite of their sin, will bring them to repentance and true change. He wants us to experience the full extent of His love, regardless of our imperfections.

I've had the privilege of visiting heaven, and see what awaits a saved person. The bottom line is that I want to live out my second chance, in the right way. Like you, I had a previous life, a past where I lived a selfish life. The Lord gave me a new chance to do things differently. To stop doing it my way, and start doing it His way!

God didn't leave me to do this on my own. He sent help in the form of His Son, Jesus, and the helper, the Holy Spirit. The same goes for every born-again believer. You will not walk this new path by your own strength, but by the help of the Lord.

Many others like myself who have died and come back, are experiencing a literal "second chance". When you speak to other people who have had similar experiences as this testimony, you will notice something different about them. They value life more. They are grateful. They have a vision to leave a lasting legacy. A legacy reflects the restoration power and love of Jesus, for all people.

I wasn't just saved from sin for my own benefit. The Lord intended me to lead others to the same freedom, the same salvation that should be experienced on a daily basis. Your salvation is alive every day. It is a living, breathing testimony that writes itself into heaven's Book of Life.

My attitude about salvation and about Jesus' impact on my life had to change. Previously, I didn't want to sell salvation to people, so I wouldn't speak about it much. I thought that people should be given the freedom to make their own choices.

But I needed to become free to share about God and the unconditional love He has for us. It wasn't about converting people at all. The Holy Spirit is responsible for conversion. It was about people experiencing the true love of the almighty God, when they encounter us. The Lord revealed the power of what His love can do. It is the power of this great love that God has for us, that brings the revelation and conversion to the hearts of people who feel lost and afraid.

This has been the message since the dawn of creation. The message has never changed! All individuals should experience the freedom of salvation, complete love, and acceptance, in Jesus Christ.

One night, the Lord gave me a dream. I was standing on Mount Carmel, overlooking the plains of Jezreel, and even up to the West bank of Israel. There was a man along-side me. In the distance, I could see civilians running. It was a time of war. The streets were lined with barb-wire. There was fighting and bombings on the outskirts. The residents were fleeing for their lives. There were young and old, parents, children, elderly, men and women, people of all cultures, colours, and religious denominations.

The soldiers were running in the opposite direction of the civilian crowds. The soldiers were shouting, "Run away! Turn back! If you go that way you will be killed!" But the crowds kept running the direction they headed in, – towards the area where the fighting was fierce. In the distance, I could see a terrible army heading their way. Fighter jets, armed with powerful missiles, were making their way to the masses. I noticed a mother running with her baby in her arms. She was heading into this terrible danger.

I turned to the man who stood along-side me, whom I now know was an angel of the Lord. In desperation, I asked the angel, "Why are these people running with their children and loved ones in the direction of this terrible danger, knowing they will be killed?"

The angel turned to me and said, "They will die for their freedom." As I looked at the angel, I then thought that at least we know God is all-powerful, and will surely save them from this calamity! The angel responded to my thoughts, saying, "This must happen, and they will die." With those words, I saw the fighter jets move in and kill the sea of innocent civilians.

I woke up, feeling angry and annoyed at this dream. *"Why had God shown me this dream?"* Years later, while spending time in prayer, the

Lord impressed on my heart, "The more people we save now, in the name of Jesus, the less will die later." He had shown me the importance of saving the souls of the lost. We need to reach the people who have not yet heard about the Lord's saving grace, who have not heard of His great love, who have not heard of His wonderful mercy.

Life is all or nothing. We shouldn't be living a life of half-measures. My new lifestyle had changed into being fully committed to become more Christ-like, driven by the passion of Christ. Respect each person as they face their challenges, because when they have victory over their obstacles, we will all benefit from it and be blessed by it.

CHAPTER 16

This Moment

Leave a legacy behind.

We only have this moment in which to live out a better life. Tomorrow is still coming and yesterday is over. Every day carries the hope of a day filled with life from God. If you want to leave a legacy behind, you may need to change the way you think about the way you approach life.

Choose to have the greatest day ever, – here and now. Nothing can stop you from wanting to be truly happy. The joy of the Lord will always be your strength, if that is what you choose. When you are doing things in your own strength, it will leave you feeling tired and drained.

Choose to make a lasting and positive difference to those you meet throughout your day. Don't worry about who you will meet tomorrow. Focus on those who are with you in this moment. You never know if this will be the last time you see each other, so let their last impression of you remain a blessed one. In your encounters with people, always ask yourself this simple question, "Were they able to see Jesus in you?"

Choose to make a beautiful impact in someone's life at this very moment. Ask the Lord, during the day, to open your eyes to the people around you; to open your heart in kindness towards them. You will find, by blessing those around you, in small or big ways, you will be uplifted. To see people smile is a great reward. Even if they cannot manage a smile or grateful response to your kindness, you have been a blessing, which will always return to you! A blessed seed must be harvested sometime in the future, and that harvest will bless you in the most unexpected way!

If this happens to be your last moment, how would you spend it? Would you spend it being angry; carrying bitterness, jealousy or un-forgiveness in your heart? No, you wouldn't, but in reality, many people choose to walk with negative issues inside their hearts. They carrying it around like an extra person, weighing them down. Take this moment to decide to deal with your issues. Present them to the Lord, and asking Him to step in and help. The sooner you do this, the sooner you will start living life the way God had intended for you. You will be released, to move forward in your life. Take this moment to choose to forgive, receive healing, restoration, and joy. Un-forgiveness makes us emotionally, or even physically ill. It steals our blessings.

> "For if you forgive men when they sin against you, your heavenly Father will also forgive you. But if you do not forgive men their sins, your Father will not forgive your sins" (Matthew 6:14-15 NIV).

Believe that there can be more goodness in your life. Many times, limitations were attached to us as we grew up. Whether these shortcomings were brought about by people, situations, or accidents, the Lord can, and will still use you, regardless. Humanity should have the desire to experience the extra-ordinary. Almighty God has placed this anticipation and hope inside of us, so we would desire to experience Him as extra-ordinary, in whichever shape or form He chooses to reveal Himself to us. The Lord doesn't want you to live a boring everyday-life. Jesus never did, so why should we? People like Moses, Joseph, Noah, Paul and Peter, all lived extraordinary lives, and so can we!

If you think you are doing well in life, challenge yourself to go one step further. When we strive for excellence in all areas, the Lord offers transformation of the highest quality! I challenge you to raise the bar, as to experience a limitless God. God is infinite, and wants you to come to know Him as the unlimited God. I challenge you to see how great you can live your life.

Take time with people. Work on your relationship with people, and with God. It is the greatest treasure you will ever own.

Remain teachable, and keep growing as a person. Learn something new. Try new things. The only way you will get to know yourself, is if you go out and experience life, experience people, and experience God in totality.

Remain humble. The Lord has a strange way of teaching us. If you lack humility, then ask the Lord to teach you more about a servant's heart. The Lord dislikes pride, because He understands what the root of pride produces in people's lives. It causes greed, an un-teachable spirit, rebellion and hate. Humility is the purest and loveliest quality God honours. It opens your eyes to the truth, doesn't exaggerate, and doesn't hurt others. With humility, wisdom is soon to follow. Only fools act with pride. Don't be a fool.

> "When pride comes, then comes disgrace, but with the humble is wisdom" (Proverbs 11:2 (ESV).

Don't be the cause of other people's destruction, or heartache. You don't want the hurt and brokenness of others, on your conscience. God can perceive your true intent. He can observe your whole life in an instant. You will find it very unpleasant to have to explain to God your cruel behaviour, towards any receiving party, whether they were friend or foe. What you thought would be your best reason to defend your selfish action, would lose its meaning in His presence.

Any act of hatred, bitterness, revenge, anger, frustration, irritation, jealousy, contempt, lust and lies, cannot stand in the presence of the

Lord. In the same way, no reason or motivation behind it will be able to stand before God. Hatred, bitterness, revenge, frustration, irritation, jealousy, contempt, lust and lies, are cultivated by the prince of lies, – Satan. They are not of God. Think twice before acting out on any of these lies.

Never judge others. None of us are aware of the life experiences of another person. We cannot even begin to understand what they have experienced, on the level of body, soul, and spirit. Only the Lord can know this. We all make mistakes, and are all worthy of forgiveness. Don't judge those who are busy dying, whether they are going to heaven or to hell. We have no real idea what kind of personal relationship they had with God. We also have no idea if God has met with them in the moments before they died, or in the few minutes after they have died.

Today, choose to become more than what you believe you are. Believe in the plan God has for your life, and start living it. The fact that God created you and set a plan in place for you, reflects His belief that you can do this. See how far you can rise above the daunting situations you may be facing. You have come this far. You are still breathing, alive, and sitting here, reading this book. While you are alive, you may as well try and live life as best you can.

No one can replace you. The world may say, "Anyone is disposable", but you are not! You are irreplaceable. God created diversity. We have no idea of the amount of diverse and multiple ways that God can love. Imagine all people that had ever existed, that are alive now, and that are still to be born, – that is only a glimpse of the diverse love that God has for mankind and His creation!

When your time comes to an end here on earth, all that you are, leaves with you. Try to finish what you have started. Leave a legacy behind that will continue to impact people long after you are gone.

CHAPTER 17

Light To The World

Dare to be a light in the darkness.

Years later after this heavenly experience, during a prayer session, the Lord revealed to me a vision of the earth in the night-time. The continents were revealed by small flames of light. These lights were not caused by electricity. Each flame had the same intensity of brightness. I asked the Lord what these lights were. He responded by revealing that all these lights represented the people on the planet. The Lord sees us as small burning lights, burning with equal intensity. No flame was bigger or brighter than the other. You couldn't tell what race or gender you were looking at. Everyone appeared the same.

I then asked the Lord, what do we sound like to Him? In an instant my mind was flooded by voices, - women, men, children, and elderly people, – all kinds of people. Not one voice was louder than another. Everyone had the same sound pitch. I heard people laughing, having fun, praying, being worried, crying, being angry, being upset, being desperate, being excited – all different states of mind.

I still couldn't categorize the people. I couldn't even identify their social status. Were they rich? Were they the president of a country? Were they living on the streets? Were they teachers?

Were they talented? Were they staying in the city? Were they staying out in the country?

To God, we are all equal and the same. He loves us all with an everlasting love. All our requests are equally important. An astonishing sight was to understand how God saw us as lights.

Just as God is the light in heaven, He wants us to represent His light here on earth. God would like us to be a light to the world.

> "The sun will no more be your light by day, nor will the brightness of the moon shine on you, for the Lord will be your everlasting light, and your God will be your glory" (Isaiah 60:19 NIV).

If each person could be represented as a candle, where the flame represents the essence of who they are, and all these candles are placed together in a group, you'll notice the amount of light that radiates from it when it is placed in a dark room. Let's say these candles represent our light in this world.

> "You are the light of the world... In the same way, let your light shine before men, that they may see your good deeds and praise your Father in heaven" (Matthew 5:14-16 NIV).

Our good deeds will bring glory to God. Your commitment to God and the way the fruit of the Holy Spirit lives in you, will determine the strength of your light in this world. The measure by which goodness, kindness, forgiveness, love, self-control, patience, and gentleness functions in you, will determine the brightness of your life in this world.

The Lord will guide you in becoming a light to the world, to reflect His light! You cannot ask for a better source of light than the Lord Himself, to teach you how to be a shining light to others.

> "Send forth your light and your truth, let them guide me; let them bring me to your holy mountain, to the place where you dwell" (Psalm 43:3 NIV).

> "The unfolding of your words gives light, it gives understanding to the simple" (Psalm 119:130 NIV).

Evil darkens the heart, while God's goodness and truth brings light into the heart. The Lord needs to be the source of your light. This power source comes in the form of the Holy Spirit. The more time you spend with the Holy Spirit the more light you will emit into the world.

> "You, O Lord, keep my lamp burning; my God turns my darkness into light" (Psalm 18:28 NIV).

Will you be a strong beacon of hope, or will your light be barely visible? Do you want the Lord to be the fuel that helps you burn for life?

When God is not our source, our light will definitely go out sooner than it should, if we choose to face our days without Him.

> This is what God the Lord says – he who created the heavens and stretched them out, who spread out the earth and all that comes out of it, who gives breath to its people, and life to those who walk on it: 'I, the Lord, have called you into righteousness; I will take hold of your hand. I will keep you and will make you to be a covenant for the people and a light for the Gentiles, to open eyes that are blind, to free captives from prison and to release from the dungeon those who sit in darkness'. (Isaiah 42:5-7 NIV)

The unity of believers cannot be stressed enough. The power that gets generated when two or more people are gathered in the name of Jesus is God-ordained. The enemy detests unity between people. He will try to destroy it every time. Satan knows he doesn't stand a change when believers are unified. The corporate covering over members of a spirit-filled church is very powerful. The angels in heaven and the demons on earth understand the power of unity in Jesus name!

Satan uses the following to cause division between believers:

- Fear
- Lies
- Deceit
- Greed
- Lust
- Pride
- Bitterness and resentment.
- Hatred
- Laziness
- Rebellion
- Stubbornness
- Distractions
- Compromise

When we are aware of these tactics, we can address them immediately. The focus must always remain on Christ, and not turn to others, or even our-selves. If it does, the enemy starts with his plan of action regarding the above-mentioned list.

Once the devil succeeds in isolating specific individuals who have started believing in his lies, they become cut off from the body of Christ. What do you think will happen to these isolated individuals?

Remember our imagery of the group of candles? Imagine removing one candle from the group, and placing it on the far side of the dark room. This single candle is isolated and alone. Its light is very dim and it may soon run out of wax or oil. It will only be moments before the slightest breath of wind could snuff it out. The candle's light will go out much quicker than in the group, and once it does, it will be surrounded by darkness.

Individuals that have isolated themselves from the body of Christ, in a similar way, will experience the same fate. Temptations will tug at them, pulling them here and there. Confusion will start creeping into their daily choices, as they move further from the truth. The world's onslaughts will be terribly hard to fight. Alone, their strength and will to live tend to diminish. Satan goes for those cut off from the source of God. The enemy focuses his attention on the easy target, where there is little resistance. The isolated person is not surrounded by a circle of friends anymore, who love them, and could pray with them, and offer spiritual protection. They are not under a protective covering of prayer any longer. This is a dangerous place to be in.

Soldiers die in wars when their equipment doesn't function properly. Soldiers are vulnerable to being wounded in battle, if they do not wear their full armour. Armies lose wars when confusion enters the camps. Armies lose wars when their units disintegrate and lose formation. Weaknesses can be exploited by the enemy, and be used to gain victory over the opposition.

When we replace certain words with the following descriptions, our paragraph above will read a little different:

- Armies – Body of Christ (Church).
- Soldiers – Believers or members of the body of Christ.
- Armour – Armour of God (Helmet of salvation; breastplate of righteousness; belt of truth; feet shod with the gospel of peace; sword of God's word; and the shield of faith).
- Equipment – Training in using the armour. Training in using the Holy Spirit. Training in understanding God's laws. Training in seeing the enemy's tactics.
- Wars – battles against Satan and his demons.
- The enemy – Satan and his demons.
- Units – unity in the church or body of Christ.

We would read the previous paragraph as follows:

> Believers die in battles against Satan and his demons, when their training is incomplete or lacking. Believers are vulnerable to being wounded in battle, if they do not wear the full armour of God. Churches lose battles against Satan and his demons, when confusion enters the camps. Churches lose battles against Satan and his demons, when their unity disintegrates and loses formation. Weaknesses can be exploited by Satan and his demons, which use it to gain victory over the opposition.

The unity of believers is a law God uses in heaven. God Himself is in unity, – God the Father, God the Son, and God the Holy Spirit, – the Trinity also works in unity, even when they function individually, in their own right.

> "The night is nearly over; the day is almost here. So let us put aside the deeds of darkness and put on the armour of light" (Romans 13:12 NIV).

To live an extraordinary life through the power of God, we need to let the Lord guide, use, and change us, into His image, into His truth and light.

PART

Practical Revelation

SECTION 4

Inherit the Whole Earth

Matthew 5:5 (NLT) "God blesses those who are humble, for they will inherit the whole earth."

CHAPTER 18

Kingdom Life

How do I change to a Kingdom lifestyle?

To live a Kingdom lifestyle, one thing must always take preference above all other things in your life, - God almighty, and His will for your life. All other things must be laid before Him. When you are able to come to the point of surrendering everything in your life, and everything that you are, to Christ, then you are able to enter into the Kingdom life.

> "But seek first the kingdom of God and His righteousness, and all these things shall be added to you" (Matthew 6:33 NKJV).

The Lord knew that once I had tasted heaven, I would never be at peace until I found it here on earth. The Holy Spirit assisted me in how to go about infusing myself with the Lord daily. It would take work from my side. Here are some basic steps that I needed to apply, and that other believers had applied in their own walk through life:

- Deal with whatever sin the Lord reveals to you.
- Grow closer to God.
- Reach out to others.

- Follow God's purpose for your life, and not what others want for you.
- Acquire a lifestyle that mirrors that of Christ Jesus.
- Speak and testify about the love of God, – plant the seed or water it. Personally I never saw any of my family in heaven. This got me thinking. I may not have planted a seed, or even watered a seed of salvation that may have turned them to Christ. I don't want any of my friends or family to miss eternal life with Christ. Do you?
- Understand the authority the Lord has given you, because you have Christ living inside of you.
- Be obedient to God at all times, regardless if you understand what He is doing or not.
- Allow the Lord to teach you through studying His word daily. It will show you the truth about what God thinks of you. It will provide guidance when you face difficult decisions.
- Spend alone time with the Lord.
- Pray every day. It will build your relationship with the Lord. Relationships die when communication ends between two people. You need to speak with the Lord, and you need to make time to listen to His voice.
- Get to know the Holy Spirit. Get to know how He works with you and leads you.
- Join a word based, spirit filled church. You need to have a solid covering of prayer over your life.
- Spend time with other fellow believers, as they will help you grow. They will cultivate love in your heart. Jesus never approached life alone. He surrounded Himself with His disciples.
- Ask the Lord for spiritual mentors, who can instruct you in God's word in every-day life. They can help introduce the power for the Holy Spirit to you, and allow you to practice the gifts of the Holy Spirit.
- Keep growing in the Lord. Year after year, evaluate your progress. Each year will be filled with its own challenges, but so too will the healing and blessing increase over your life, and

over the lives of those you love. Never stop learning. You can never know enough.

- Be willing to change. We are all being shaped by God on a continual basis. You will get to know yourself as the Lord reveals it to you.
- Surrender all things that keep you from getting closer to the Lord.
- Surrender all things that stop you from growing.
- Surrender all the things that may keep God from using you.
- Surrender all the hurts and pain, so all your wounds can heal, and your soul can become whole.

Don't delay in any of these above-mentioned points. The enemy loves it when we are lazy and stagnant. That is when he decides to strike. Don't allow him to get the slightest foothold in your life.

Rise up to this new way of life. Be excited and be brave. You will never want to turn back once you have seen what wonderful miracles can take place. Change gives us the opportunity to prove that the extraordinary is possible in one's life. Become extraordinary, by the power and the love of God.

> "Ah, Lord God! Behold, You have made the heavens and the earth by Your great power and outstretched arm. There is nothing too hard for You ..." (Jeremiah 32:18 NKJV)

All things are possible through Christ Jesus, the Son of the living God! When people say that you may never be able to turn your life around, don't believe them. The truth is that you can! Your past has nothing to do with the devil, or anyone else for that matter. It is between you and God alone. All people are capable of changing into someone beautiful, powerful, and blessed. Everyone has a past, but all people have the possibility of a beautiful future.

***

Note to the reader: The next few chapters are pretty intense. They may take you days to work through, as it digs into your persona. These chapters will raise questions about who you are, and who you want to become. Take your time, there is no rush. The Lord wants to work on the state of your heart and your mind. Give Him a chance to do this for you, and with you.

CHAPTER 19

Words

The power to create and the power to destroy.

The Lord is always gentle in the way He teaches and instructs us. The Holy Spirit also assists us with bringing wisdom and understanding to the Lord's instruction. The following is what the Lord Jesus revealed about *words.*

Words – The power to create and the power to destroy.

- What kind of words come out of our mouths on a daily basis? What does it sound like to the people who hear them?
- What kind of words do we utter over ourselves and over other people?
- Are our words specifically chosen according to whom we are speaking to? (If it is friends, family, leaders, people in your care, even your enemies)
- Are our words kind and powerful, bringing restoration, encouragement, and instruction? Or are they destructive and insensitive, causing brokenness, sadness, pain, or hurt over other people? (Things like this only lead to lies, anger and regret anyway.)
- Do we speak words of regret?
- Are there words you wish you had spoken, but didn't?

- Do our words echo truth?
- Do our words draw the true picture of us, or the wrong picture of us?
- Are our words deceiving, or are they pure?
- Do our words heal, or do they bruise the one listening?

> "By the Word of the Lord were the heavens made and all their hosts by the breath of his mouth" (Psalm 33:6 AMP).

Words are a very important item on God's list. God spoke creation into being. God even said in the Bible that He cannot go against His own promises which He had spoken over us.

> "So God has given both his promise and his oath. These two things are unchangeable because it is impossible for God to lie" (Hebrews 6:18-19 NLT).

God actually values words to such an extent, that His Son, Jesus Christ, became the living Word, by which all things were created and spoken into existence.

> "In the beginning was the Word, and the Word was with God, and the Word was God. He was in the beginning with God. All things came into being through Him, and apart from Him nothing came into being that has come into being" (John 1:1-3 AMP).

Jesus, who was the Word its self, spoke the word. He knew and understood the power of the spoken word. He was careful in what He said. When Jesus spoke, it was with power and authority.

> "Then He arose and rebuked the wind and said to the sea, "Peace, be still!". And the wind ceased and there was a great calm" (Mark 4:39 ESV).

If God can create with spoken words, we can do the same with our words. Even the devil understands this. There is power in the tongue. There is power in the words you speak over yourself, your children, your friends, your families, strangers and even your enemies. Personally, we all understand the impact words have on our heart and spirit. Words have a lasting impression on people, and it plants a seed in the heart of the listener.

> "But what comes out of the mouth proceeds from the heart, and this defiles a person" (Matthew 15:18 ESV).

The book of Proverbs speaks a lot about what comes out of people's mouths. What truly resides in your heart? Have you listened lately to what you have been saying? I think most of us would be shocked to hear what comes out of our mouths. We may even be ashamed to see what it reveals about our hearts. It's easy to speak because anyone can do that, but it takes practice to hear your own words in the way other people would hear it. If you could hear what you are about to say, you would probably think twice about voicing it.

For some people, words are their weapons to use when they intend to hurt others. God has a stern warning about this in the Bible.

> "But I say to you that for every idle word men may speak, they will give account of it in the day of judgement. For by your words you will be justified, and by your words you will be condemned" (Matthew 12:36-37 NKJV).

Even when you want to hurt others by your words, you will be hurting yourself. That is how curses work. When you curse others, you open the workings of that same curse over yourself. Also, when you choose to speak a blessing over people, even over your enemies, you release that same blessing over yourself.

The Lord once gave me a vision of a wall covered in an array of beautiful swords. He pointed at some swords and told me that He loved those and would like me to keep them. Then He pointed to some other swords which also appeared beautiful, but He wanted me to get rid of them. The Lord said that the swords represented all the different words I spoke. There were some words He liked, but there were others He instructed me to stop using. And so I did.

The words I needed to stop using were words of jealousy, insult, false accusation, negativity, anger, pride, selfishness, ugliness, and lies. The words He wanted me to keep using were words of truth, kindness, goodness, encouragement, love, forgiveness, and life. Does this sound familiar to you?

Believe me, whatever comes out of your mouth, you will have to take responsibility for, in some shape or form. Think before you speak. Let the Lord lead your words, but most importantly, let Him change your heart, so your words will change automatically. It is far better to be the echo of life to someone's troubled ears, than to be the sound of destruction and death.

> "You have tested my thoughts and examined my heart in the night. You have scrutinized me and found nothing wrong. I am determined not to sin in what I say" (Psalm 17:3 NLT).

To change one's words becomes a life-long project, – practise, listen, and learn from your verbal mistakes. Some days you succeed, and other days you will fail. The more you work at it, the more you change, and the more blessings will be evident in your life.

Your challenge for this Chapter:

- Take note of what comes out your mouth each time you speak to someone. Then listen to what comes out of the other person's mouth in the conversation. Is it positive or negative?

- Make a mental note each time you catch yourself gossiping.

- Make a mental note each time you are bad-mouthing someone else.

- Make a mental note when you find yourself telling a fib, a white lie, or even a genuine proper lie.

- When spending time with God, make a note of what it is you are saying to Him. Are you asking things all the time? Are you complaining? Are you thankful or grateful?

All of these challenges are to help you see what you are speaking over your life, and over the lives of others. Then you need to ask the question: "Why am I doing this and how can I change it if it is not good?"

Here is a tip - The Word of God is the best place to start when you are in need of a new way of speaking.

CHAPTER 20

Thoughts

The power that shapes your perception of everything.

What the heart is filled with, the mouth will usually run over with. (Matthew 15:18) The one question you may have towards the Lord is this: "If I am speaking inappropriately, how do I change it?" The Lord will probably simply ask in turn: "What are your daily thoughts like?" The Lord Jesus revealed the following about *thoughts*.

Thoughts – The power that shapes your perception of everything.

- What kind of thoughts do we have about ourselves, about other people and about God?
- What thoughts and lies do we allow the devil to shape in our minds, so we end up believing it?
- Do we have our own thoughts, or do we allow people and events, to shape our thinking?
- Do our thoughts uplift us, or weigh us down?
- Does it scare us to be alone with our thoughts?
- Are we afraid of what other people think of us?
- Do we fear what God must think of us?

Many times we think the worst about ourselves. We think people think terrible things about us. We may even assume God thinks the worst of us too. Even if people do – that is their issue, *but God only has good thoughts towards us.*

> "'For I know the thoughts that I think towards you', says the Lord, 'thoughts of peace (wholeness, well being, health, blessing) and not of evil, to give you a future and a hope'." (Jeremiah 29:11 NKJV)

All the Lord wants is for us to have the same thoughts about ourselves, as He has about us. In the same way He wants our thoughts about other people, to be the same as His thinking about them.

- Do you know what God thinks about you?
- Do you know what God thinks about the people in your life?
- Do you know what God thinks about the strangers you meet daily?
- Do you know what God thinks about your enemies?

> In Jeremiah 29 it says the Lord has thoughts of peace for you and me, not evil. The Lord's thoughts want to give us a future and a hope. In my own life I had to ask the question like this:

- Jeanne, do you have peaceful thoughts about yourself? Is there anger and bitterness in your heart towards yourself, which darkens your thoughts?
- Jeanne, do you have peaceful thoughts towards your friends, family and even your enemies? Are your thoughts towards them vengeful, filled with bitterness, resentment, jealousy, and discontentment?

The truth is, when un-forgiveness, hurt, resentment, and anger lingers in our thoughts, there is no space for the thoughts of God. The enemy loves a ship-wrecked mind with no direction or stability. He can play with your mind, emotions and your health. The enemy does this by lying to you, deceiving and tricking you into believing the worst of any situation. When you don't know God's word, which is the truth, your mind becomes a battlefield.

Our thinking affects our daily perception of life and the world we live in. What am I saying? I'm saying, when we lose perspective, our world falls apart, - our minds fall apart. This happens because we do not know the truth, and we do not live in the truth. Jesus faced His own mind-battles in two well known instances.

The one was in the wilderness, for 40 days:

> "Then Jesus was led by the Spirit into the wilderness to be tempted by the devil. After fasting forty days and forty nights ..." (Matthew 4:1 NIV)

Jesus countered the onslaughts of the devil by quoting God's word. Jesus spoke these words because He meditated on them while growing up, making them a part of His thought-life. In doing so, Jesus had the thoughts and words He needed on the days it mattered most. The devil himself couldn't say anything against Jesus.

> "Jesus answered, "It is written: 'Man shall not live on bread alone, but on every word that comes from the mouth of God.'" " (Matthew 4:4 NIV)

The second place where Jesus faced a mind-battle was in the Garden of Gethsemane, in the evening hours before He was captured:

> "Then Jesus went with His disciples to a place called Gethsemane ..." (Matthew 26:36 NIV)

The same principle applies here. Jesus had hidden God's thoughts about Him in His heart. This gave Jesus the ability to pray the prayer He did in the garden.

> "'Abba, Father', he said, 'everything is possible for you. Take this cup from me. Yet not what I will, but what you will.' " (Mark 14:36 NIV)

In both instances, Jesus knew the truth, because He knew God's word and understood God's thoughts about Him.

The only way to beat negativity, the onslaughts of depression, and despair, is to fill your mind with the word of God. The word of God is packed with power and hope. Whenever dark thoughts rise up in your mind, you can be assured that those scriptures you have been meditating on will come up in your spirit, to wash away the darkness in your mind. You may ask, "How is this possible? Why would this work where everything else you have tried has failed?" The answer is this: God's word is alive and gives life to those who hear it, speak it, believe it, do it, and carry it in their hearts.

Changing your thoughts to the way God thinks, will change everything for you. It will change:

... the way you pray to God;
... the way you pray for yourself;
... the way you pray for people;
... the way you speak to God;
... the way you speak about people;
... the way you speak to people, etc.

If you are able to bless people and bless your enemies, by the way you pray for, and think about them, those seeds of blessing will come back to enrich your life. However, if you speak a curse, and carry hate and bitterness in your heart, the only person you destroy is yourself.

> "Search me, O God, and know my heart; test me and know my anxious thoughts. Point out anything in me that offends you, and lead me along the path of everlasting life" (Psalm 139:23-24 NLT).

Start thinking the way you would like to start speaking. If you want your words to carry power, life and beauty, your thoughts need to be the first place to reflect this change. Your thoughts are the store-houses for change. Allow the Lord to show you what needs to change, and how to do this. Every person is ever-changing. When you cease transformation into the image of Christ, then you know you are heading for disaster.

The enemy may even come and whisper in your ear, "You don't have to change for anyone. God's word says He loves you just the way you are." This is deception! Yes, God loves us just as we are, but we need to change from a sinful nature and embrace the character of Christ Jesus, – this signifies change. It means walking away from the old bad habits, and replacing them with holy, godly ways.

God treasures you enough to think about you every second of your existence. Don't forget how important you are to Him. What a beautiful example God's thoughts are, concerning how we ought to think about each other, and about ourselves.

We have no idea what other people are experiencing, or going through in their personal lives. Start thinking about the people around you, and let God lead you in this.

Ask the Lord what His thoughts might be on the specific person you are thinking of. You will be surprised at what comes up in your heart. God will teach you how to take note of people, and how not to take them for granted.

> "What is man that You are mindful of him, and the son of man that You visit him? For You have made him a little lower than the angels, and You have crowned him with glory and honour" (Psalm 8:4 NKJV).

Your challenge for this Chapter:

- Make a mental note each time you catch yourself thinking negatively throughout the day.

- Make a mental note each time you catch yourself thinking positively throughout the day.

- When observing people during the day, take note of what you are thinking about them. Is it what God would think?

- When spending time with God, make a note of what it is you are thinking regarding Him.

All of these challenges are to help you observe what your mind is occupied with. Next you need to ask the question: "Why is my mind so preoccupied with these things and how can I change it if it is not good?"

Here is a tip - Use the Bible to teach you a new way of thinking.

CHAPTER 21

Motives

The power that steers your actions.

The Lord does not rush into sharing revelation with people. He tends to work systematically, orderly, in a way for humanity to keep up with His awesome wisdom. In saying this, let us look at the next item the Lord wants us to pay attention to in our lives.

Chapter 20 addressed the questions the Lord raised around what our thinking was like on a daily basis. The Lord then moved on and pointed to my heart. A new significant question developed, "What is hidden in our hearts that causes us to think the way we do? Are our hearts filled with truth, or with lies and deception?" The following is what the Lord Jesus revealed about *motives.*

Motives – The power that steers your actions.

- What are our motives for doing something?
- What are our intentions when starting relationships with people?
- What are our motives for going to church?
- What are our intentions for each action?
- What are the motives behind our prayers?

If I had to ask you to voice the true intentions of your heart, would you be worried, ashamed, nervous, or defensive? Or wouldn't you mind at all to share the hidden motives in your heart?

Mankind has always had reasons for doing things and acting in certain ways. Even God has had reasons for creating, doing, and acting in various ways. An action is always the result of a justified reason, or motive.

> "Put me on trial, Lord, and cross-examine me. Test my motives and my heart" (Psalm 26:2 NLT).

When last did you examine your heart? Sometimes we are so busy living, we never stop to think of the real purpose behind the things we are busy with. If once in a while, we do not take time out to look at our own hearts, and what is happening in them, wrong motives creep in unnoticed.

After some time, these incorrect motives start twisting good intentions into selfish looking reasons. After a while, you have become the very person you never wanted to be; self-absorbed and chasing after false happiness. You even end up using people for your own selfish purposes without even noticing it. Pride takes hold of your soul, and it all goes downhill from there.

Motives are a very important and powerful item the Lord wants to expose and discuss. He knows that in our intentions, rests the potential for evil to transpire in the world. Please understand how important this is. If self-seeking motives are practiced regularly, pride follows instantaneously.

In heaven, Lucifer was once the angel of music. God saw the motive in Lucifer's heart. Pride alone threatened the purity of Lucifer's actions towards God. Pride alone threatened his actions towards his fellow angels in heaven. Deceit, pride, and self-exaltation, had risen in Lucifer's heart. (Isaiah 14:13-15) In heaven there is no place for this, for God is the only one to be glorified and placed on high.

> "The Lord supports the humble, but He brings the wicked down into the dust" (Psalm 147:6 NLT).

> "For the Lord delights in His people; He crowns the humble with victory" (Psalm 149:4 NLT).

God made a universal example of Lucifer, regarding pride and humility, because God knows the devastating implications pride carries. The Bible tells us that the Lord delights in those who are humble. They are seen as His people, and He will crown them with victory. He will support them and rescue them, but the wicked He will humiliate and bring down.

> "God blesses those who are humble, for they will inherit the whole earth" (Matthew 5:5 NLT).

God clearly states His promise to the humble in the above scripture. This is a beautiful promise; the humble will inherit all the earth, - all the beauty of the waters, the land, the animals on the land, in the water, and in the air, - all of it.

One day, you will come to stand before God. No one will stand with you, - not your friends, your family, or even those people you may have blamed for your choices. You will personally take responsibility for the way you conducted your life, whether it was righteous or unrighteous.

> "For we speak as messengers approved by God to be entrusted with the Good News. Our purpose is to please God, not people. He alone examines the motives of our hearts" (1 Thessalonians 2:4 NLT).

Your soul and your heart belong solely to you. The "free will" God gave to you to make choices with, belongs to you alone. It doesn't even belong to God. The price of this freedom is that the sole responsibility for decisions will fall on the individual. We cannot blame or point fingers at anyone but ourselves for the choices we make in life. You cannot even blame God.

However, in some cases, people get damaged by others or circumstances, resulting in a broken mind, and a broken spirit. They could not withstand the onslaughts of the enemy. These broken people may end up hurting others. Regardless of this, the depth of God's grace and mercy towards these people, go beyond our understanding. The power of restoration through God is immeasurable.

Christ's righteousness that lives on the inside of a broken individual, can bring forgiveness and eternal life. The Lord's grace on those wounded souls, who are unable to choose accordingly, fall under God's wise counsel. We cannot judge the motives of other people. We can only be held responsible for our own motives. Our own restoration lay with the willingness to want to heal and become whole.

> "The purpose of my instruction is that all believers would be filled with love that comes from a pure heart, a clean conscience, and genuine faith" (1Timothy 1:5 NLT).

A powerful person is someone with a pure heart, with good intentions, rooted in love. The Lord honours a person with a clear conscience. Prayers become more powerful and a person's life becomes more blessed. Your mind becomes protected from polluted thoughts. Once the Lord has the space to live freely in your mind and in your heart, burdens will lift and you experience a freedom that cannot be taken from you. Even kings will recognise you and allow you in their presence.

> "Whoever loves a pure heart and gracious speech will have the king as a friend" (Proverbs 22:2 NLT).

Your life journey will be riddled with all kinds of challenges. I pray that you will always find time to pursue the challenge of striving for a holier and purified lifestyle. The treasure of having an intimate relationship with God walks hand in hand with holiness and purity. God is holy and pure.

> "... Instead, pursue righteous living, faithfulness, love, and peace. Enjoy the companionship of those who call on the Lord with pure hearts" (2 Timothy 2:22 NLT).

Keep in mind that you do not have to attempt this lifestyle change in your own strength and power. The Lord will be there to help you. Christ's righteousness that lives inside of you makes this possible.

When King David had failed and made mistakes, he knew that only God would be able to salvage the situation and save his soul in the process. King David also knew that these challenges would strengthen his relationship with the living God. Instead of allowing his sin to push him away from God, King David chose to allow his mistakes to draw him closer to God. Do the same in your walk with God.

> "Create in me a clean heart, O God. Renew a loyal spirit within me" (Psalm 51:10 NLT).

God is not going anywhere, even when it feels like He is. Usually, we are the ones that pull away when sin occurs in our lives. In the Garden of Eden, Adam and Eve were hiding away from God when they had sinned. God wasn't the one pulling away. In fact, He went looking for them. He knew full well what they had done, but His love for them would still provide the grace they needed to continue living.

Your challenge for this Chapter:

- Make a list of all the projects you are currently busy with. Then jot down the reasons why you are doing them.

- Make a list of all the friends you currently have. Then give a real reason why you have them in your life.

- Think back on all those friends you no longer have. Think of the reasons why they were in your life, and why they are no longer in your life.

- Make a list of family members. Then write down what your motives have been with each one of them.

All of these challenges are to help reveal the truth in your heart and the state of your soul. What are the motives behind your friendships and actions? Are you currently in a good place, or are you wondering around in dark, dangerous territory. Then you need to ask the questions: "Do I want to be in this state? Am I happy being this type of person? How did I get here? And if I don't like what I see, how can I change it?"

Here is a tip - Ask the Lord to show you the truth regarding your motives.

CHAPTER 22

Actions

The visible power of the truth in your heart.

"Practice what you preach", is probably one of the most well-known sayings in the world, because it is so true. The world is so used to people breaking their promises. Whether they are leaders, workers, friends, or family, it is every human being's responsibility to take action when need be.

God has always been a God of miracles, action, creativity, and wonder. Jesus Christ, God's Son, was known to do the same. When Jesus walked the earth, He was a living representation of God's word. To the Lord, actions represent the physical application of one's word. The following is what the Lord Jesus revealed about *actions.*

Actions – The visible power of the truth in your heart.

- Do our actions line up with what we say?
- Do our actions line up with our intentions? Can people trust our actions? Or do we have hidden motives behind them?
- What do our actions say about us?
- If we made a promise to someone, do we actually follow through on our promise?
- Do we procrastinate in some areas where we should be actively doing something?

- Are our actions harmful to ourselves?
- Are our actions harmful to others?
- What do our actions reflect about our hearts towards God?

> "There is no greater love than to lay down one's life for one's friends" (John 15:13 NLT).

Christ said to His disciples that there was no greater love than to sacrifice one's life for a friend. Christ then gave up His own life and was crucified for all of us, – an action that proved His words to be true. Jesus practised what He preached.

> "You see that his faith and his actions were working together, and his faith was made complete by what he did" (James 2:22 NIV).

If you have something to say, make sure it is backed up with real deeds and actions that will prove you truthful. Don't be fooled to think your actions won't make you out to be a liar, if they do not line up with what you say. Some people are born with an eloquent tongue, but their speech is untrustworthy and misleading. Our actions will always reflect what the mind and heart are truly busy with.

> "Our actions will show that we belong to the truth, so we will be confident when we stand before God" (1 John 3:19 NLT).

People will start trusting you more when they see your actions are in line with what you say. Will you ever follow a leader who makes empty promises? No, if there are no real results from that leader, you will search for another who follows through with deeds. Empty promises lead nowhere!

> "They saw the works of the Lord, his wonderful deeds in the deep" (Psalm 107:24 NIV).

People saw that Jesus was a man of His word. God, Himself, has always been a God of action. He always keeps a promise, in word and deed.

> "Oh, that my actions would consistently reflect your decrees!" (Psalm 119:5 NLT)

If you and I were created in the image of God, wouldn't it be true to say that our words and deeds should carry the same weight and quality as that of God Himself? If Christ is living in me, I would want to share His nature, - to act and behave as He would.

> "You said, 'I will reign forever as queen of the world!' You did not reflect on your actions or think about the consequences" (Isaiah 47:7 NLT).

The scripture in Isaiah is an important observation about taking responsibility for the way we act. How many times have you ever really thought about an action before you did it? Often you may find yourself overreacting in a situation before thinking it through. You may be too quick to react, when you should have stepped back for a moment and considered the bigger picture.

> "Commit your actions to the Lord, and your plans will succeed" (Proverbs 16:3 NLT).

When Christ is at the centre of everything; at the centre of your thoughts, intentions, your heart, and the centre of your life; your deeds will show this and fall in line with the blessing of success. Stop doing things your way, and start doing things God's way. He is the true formula to success, peace, and joy.

Our actions will reveal patterns throughout our lives. At times, patterns of destruction become apparent as you take account of the recurring moments in your life, - such as hurtful relationships, addictions, wrong jobs, and wrong living environments, etc. Sometimes it may seem as though you are stuck in one place in your life, absent of any progress, blessing, success, or happiness.

Commitment is one of the most renowned actions people struggle with. Some individuals cannot keep their commitments, or are afraid to commit to something. Fear is the main cause for individuals to not commit. Fear is not of God. The Bible tells us that we have been given a spirit of power, hope, and a sound mind. We have not been given a spirit of fear.

If you struggle with completing things you have started, enquire with the Lord to show you why this is happening. There could be many reasons:

- You may feel your feats won't change anything;
- You are afraid of committing to something that won't work out, or that it won't last because of preconceived fears;
- It may feel daunting to act upon that which you had promised;
- You may feel inadequately equipped for the expected action you need to perform;
- Your attitude needs some adjusting in the sense of changing your focus from yourself, on to your fellow-man.

Whatever the reason may be, there is always a root to these kinds of matters that need restoration. There is no use in attending to the symptoms, if the real issue is not dealt with. This is what the Lord specializes in, – complete and thorough healing in the hearts of His children.

Your challenge for this Chapter:

- List the times you made a promise to someone, but you didn't follow through with it.

- List the times you made a promise to God, but you didn't follow through with it.

- From the above lists, write down why you think you didn't go through with the promises.

- Make a list of the things you have done in life that didn't work out. In hindsight, do you think you thought things through before acting on it? Did you consult God? Did you decide to follow your own head instead of listening to good advice, or God's leading?

- List those things you always speak of, but need to put into action, – in other words, to actually do what you said you were going to do.

All of these challenges are to help you find out if you have any patterns of destruction. This exercise is also intended to help you understand why it is that you cannot keep commitments? If you want people to trust you, you need to be honest about your actions. If you want to be able to trust yourself, you need to be honest with yourself too. Sometimes we need to take a step back and regain perspective of our lives.

This section also investigates why it is that you don't follow through with ideas, or struggle to finish projects once you have started them.

Here is a tip - Ask a loyal and truthful friend to sit with you regarding the actions you are struggling with in your life. Work through each item on the list and pray about it together.

CHAPTER 23

Relationship

The power to grow.

God is all about relationship. Never did I realize how important this was to God until this moment. The misconception of God is caused by confusion brought about by the diverse religions worldwide.

God is not about religion. He is all about relationship. In the same breath I can say Jesus and the Holy Spirit are also all about relationship. The following is what the Lord Jesus revealed about *relationship.*

Relationship – The power to grow.

- What kind of relationships do we have with our family and friends?
- What kind of relationship do we have with God?
- Are we too busy with our own lives to make time to get to know others and God better?
- Do we want to get to know people?
- Are we afraid to build relationships, in the fear of exposing our own hearts, and risk caring more about others than ourselves?

> "Yes, a person is a fool to store up earthly wealth but not have a rich relationship with God" (Luke 12:21 NLT).

Relationships are more precious than worldly possessions. Things cannot love you, bring utter joy to your life, bring you laughter, offer you support and comfort, or show mercy and forgiveness. Only people can. Only the Lord can. The empty void inside of us can only be filled by the love of God. Experiencing this love comes from a relationship with Him. Yes, people may hurt and disappoint us, but God will never disappoint. In fact, when you have a living relationship with the Lord, He will bring healing to those areas where others have hurt you, just so you can love them again. We have to forgive to be able to love again. God wired us in such a way to desire love and show love.

> "So now we can rejoice in our new relationship with God because our Lord Jesus Christ has made us friends of God" (Romans 5:11 NLT).

God the Father is in relationship with His Son, Jesus, and the Holy Spirit. Jesus Christ is in relationship with the Father God and Holy Spirit. And the Holy Spirit is in relationship with Jesus Christ and God the Father. The trinity understands the importance of relationship. We can also have a similar relationship, when we have Jesus Christ living on the inside of us.

> "Then Jesus cried out, 'Whoever believes in me does not believe in me only, but in the one who sent me. The one who looks at me is seeing the one who sent me'." (John 12:44-45 NIV)

When Jesus was baptised by John, all three were present, - God the Father and the Holy Spirit. This is a beautiful example of Christ Jesus flowing in the will of His Father, God, and the Holy Spirit coming down to empower Jesus. It is the ultimate expression of love in the trinity.

> One day Jesus came from Nazareth in Galilee, and John baptized him in the Jordan River. As Jesus came up out

> of the water, he saw the heavens splitting and the Holy Spirit descended on him like a dove. And a voice from heaven said, 'You are my dearly loved Son, and you bring me great joy.' (Mark 1:9-11 NLT)

We were created for relationships. Since the beginning of time, God wanted relationship with humanity. Think of Adam and Eve in the garden. They had long walks with God. Remember God's relationship with Abraham, Moses, Joseph, David, etc. God so much wanted a relationship with us, and He disliked the separation caused by sin.

> "Yes, Adam's one sin brings condemnation for everyone, but Christ's one act of righteousness brings a right relationship with God and new life for everyone" (Romans 5:18 NLT).

God had a plan to resolve this. His plan was Jesus Christ who would die on the cross for our sins so we could come into the right relationship with God again.

> "They will receive the Lord's blessing and have a right relationship with God their Saviour" (Psalm 24:5 NLT).

Every relationship I ever had on earth became a part of me in heaven; the way I treated people; the way I spoke to them; the way I loved them; the way I cared for them. What I knew about them, and what they had brought alive in my own heart, became a part of me. I could see how much I had grown from all the relationships I had in my life, – both the good and the not so good relationships. I never realized the extent of fullness I would feel from the love people gave me in my life. I never realized the extent of complete love I would experience from God. It was most unexpected.

You can never realize the impact you make in an individual's life, until you journey to heaven or to hell. By then it is too late. I hope you take note of these words and cement them into your heart. Your every relationship with children, parents, friends, family, strangers, and even your enemies, is carried with you into eternity. Their presence in your life, affects your spirit and your heart, regardless if you loved them or not. Your presence in their lives affects their spirit and their heart.

If you have been running away from relationship issues, believe me, you will come to face them in the here-after. In heaven, you keep growing and learning. It doesn't stop just because your body has died. The learning continues in heaven.

When all the external influences are stripped away, and you only have your soul left, which is the essence of your being, you will find treasures there which you were never aware of:

- treasures of love,
- peace,
- forgiveness,
- unending joy,
- grace,
- mercy,
- freedom.

In heaven, these treasures are all exposed, while on earth they are hidden away in our hearts. While we are alive here on earth, the trick is to expose and surface the beautiful treasures in ourselves, and use them in relationships. When Christ lives inside of you, it is easier to do this, because these represent the characteristics of Jesus Himself.

On earth, we experience a fallen world and a fallen nature, – hate, anger, jealousy, rebellion, bitterness, rejection, etc. These negative characteristics make us insecure and vulnerable in the wrong way. Unnatural boundaries form in our lives, separating us from God's love and the love of others. Our relationships with people and even God become fragile and shaky, and may even break up. This is the very thing God didn't intend for us.

The enemy causes fear in our lives to prevent us from reaching out and building relationships. He will even cause distractions that blind us into false security, like the following:

- Living for ourselves;
- We think with money we will be secure;
- We convince ourselves that if we have power, no one can hurt us;
- We try to do things for others in the hope that they might love us more; etc.

Does this sound familiar? When the enemy separates you from having relationships with well-grounded people, and if he is able to push you away from God by means of lies; you get into deeper, more dangerous waters. That is when trouble arises. You stop growing in the right direction, and may even think you know everything. This is called, pride and false wisdom. Pride starts to smother your proper thinking.

As humans, we find it so easy to judge, blame, and criticize other people. Even God Himself bears the brunt of our judgemental thoughts. It is immature. The enemy uses this tactic to alienate you from God, and from good people. When you make the effort to get to know a person, or to get to know God personally, you start to realize who they truly are. I learned to watch my judgmental thoughts. It was wiser to rather focus working on my own short comings and character, than to focus on others. Stop trying to be more right than the next person. Rather, compare your own life to the Lord's word, using it as your own measuring stick in your own journey to change.

A person cannot be held responsible for other people's growth. You can only be held responsible for your own. Being in relationship with our fellow-man, and with God, helps us grow. It teaches us the following:

- How to forgive;
- How to love unconditionally;
- How to be merciful;
- How to be humble;
- How to listen;
- How to be selfless;
- How to accept others and their uniqueness.

Start building a relationship with the people around you. Get to know them. Really show some interest in their lives. Allow them to touch your heart, and help you grow as an individual. Diversity is wonderful. Don't be afraid of it. Diversity allows you to learn more about yourself, and come to love all the different parts of yourself. In the same way, you will grow to love each person for their individuality. God is a God of diversity, and He would love for you to discover all the different kinds of people He has created.

We experience our ups and downs, regarding relationships with people, but when we have a relation with God, healing and restoration is possible on all levels of our relationships. This includes our relationship with Him.

> "Anyone who wanders away from His teaching has no relationship with God. But anyone who remains in the teaching of Christ has a relationship with both the Father and the Son" (2 John 1:9 NLT).

To build a relationship with God means you need to spend time with Him. Spend time in prayer and in the Word, - the Bible. Get to know Him. Don't just listen and accept what people say about God. Go straight to the Bible and find out for yourself. Spend time in prayer, where God will start speaking to you. This way you will grow in relationship with God the Father, His Son Jesus Christ, and the Holy Spirit.

> "Clearly, God's promise to give the whole earth to Abraham and his descendants was based not on his obedience to God's law, but on a right relationship with God that comes by faith" (Romans 4:13 NLT).

The Lord has so many beautiful promises in His word, regarding your life. Most importantly, they all belong to you, because you are in relationship with Him. When you are in relationship with God, the overpowering love He has for you, changes you to such an extent that you would rather listen and obey His words, than follow your own mind-set. Your own self-centred ways will become pointless.

Your challenge for this Chapter:

- Do you have good relationships with people? How would you rate them? Is there room for improvement?

- Do you have a relationship with God, or do you see it as a religious activity? Do you see God as near to you, or far away and not really a part of your daily walk?

- List the reasons why you may be afraid of relationships?

- What do you love about relationships?

- Are you growing in your relationships with the people in your life?

- Are you growing in your relationship with God?

- Do you think people in your life grow because of your relationship with them?

All of these challenges are to help you find out what kind of relationships you have cultivated with people, and with God, over the years. You may have to work on your relationship skills, or you may be on the right track. It is a good idea to annually take inventory regarding your associations. It will show you if you are growing in the right direction, if you are stuck in one place, or if you are heading for danger.

Here is a tip - Ask the Lord to reveal to you the truth in this subject of relationships. Let Him help you change and grow.

CHAPTER 24

Focus

The power of a Christ-centred life.

The Lord Jesus Christ walked the earth with focus and purpose. He did only what the Father asked of Him. He did not follow His own desires. Jesus was not busy doing His own thing.

God is a God of order, not chaos. Jesus' own life was a perfect example of this. He wasn't running around all over the place, keeping Himself occupied with distractions. God used His Son wherever He was at that moment, and when God spoke to Him, Jesus moved. The Lord shared the following regarding *focus.*

Focus - The power of a Christ-centred life.

- What are we focusing on?
- Are we focusing on the wellbeing, or destruction, of our family, friends, co-workers, or other people?
- Is work our main focus?
- Does money, success, and possessions, preoccupy our minds?
- Is our focus on our addictions, whatever they may be?
- Is our focus on our sins, the temptations out there, or other immoral things?
- Are we attracted to the counterfeit this world has to offer?

- Has our focus been on holiness, goodness, kindness, and excellence?
- Has our focus been on Christ and His kingdom?

Life itself can be a distraction for us. What do I mean when I say this? Relationships, work, health, finances, etc., can keep a person's mind and heart preoccupied from the things of God. At times, a person may not even realize when their focus has become disrupted. Without noticing, the individual wanders away from their focal point in life, heading in the opposite direction.

The Lord teaches us that there is a general rule to check whether your focus is correct. You can be assured you are heading for disaster, when your focus is not entirely on the Lord, or His kingdom.

> "... How I have been grieved by their adulterous hearts, which have turned away from me, and by their eyes, which have lusted after their idols. They will loathe themselves for the evil they have done and for all their detestable practices" (Ezekiel 6:8-9 NIV).

Whenever we place anything before God, it becomes an idol in our lives. A simple example, - you may place your money-worries before your time with God (you would rather spend your time worrying, than spending actual time in God's presence, seeking guidance); or you spend more time with your family than with God. Even these seemingly 'good things', can become idols when we place them above God.

> "You shall have no other gods before me. You shall not make for yourself an idol in the form of anything in heaven above or on the earth beneath or in the waters below" (Exodus 20:3-4 NIV).

Why is God saying this? It is to protect us. We lose the blessing and fullness of life, when we worship and glorify things. We lose the blessing and fullness of life, when we idolize people, whom have no way of measuring up to godly perfection. This reverence, perfection, and honour, belongs solely to God almighty. Not even angels are to be worshiped.

> "But seek first the kingdom of God and His righteousness, and all these things will be added to you" (Matthew 6:33 ESV).

When our attention ultimately turns to the Lord, we are saying that we trust God completely as our provider, our King, our friend, our comforter, our protector, our healer. As we keep our focus on God, we give Him the power to take care of all the things we cannot take care of.

> "In everything you do, put God first, and He will direct you and crown your efforts with success." (Proverbs 3:6 TLB)

The Lord wants us to take this step of faith and place Him first in all we do. When we have a beautiful purpose and reason for doing something, our focus will become sharper, greater, and more powerful. If the Lord becomes your reason for:

- Studying
- Working
- Cleaning
- Serving
- Cooking
- Drawing
- Making music
- Singing
- Building
- Training
- Loving others
- Forgiving others...

> ... Then your existence and your purpose take on a whole new meaning.

When Peter was in the boat with the other disciples, they saw Jesus walking towards them on the water. Jesus called out to Peter to get out of the boat and walk towards Him. Peter, in faith, did this, and was walking on the water towards Jesus. As Peter took his eyes off Jesus and turned his attention to the waves, his faith waivered and he sank into the water. The Lord was there to pull him out. Jesus asked Peter why he doubted.

When we allow our eyes to turn away from the waves and onto the Lord, our attention will follow. Once our awareness is on the Lord, things start changing and miracles start happening. We think more clearly, and realize the Lord's hand is in everything.

> "For those who will live according to the flesh set their minds on the things of the flesh, but those who live according to the Spirit set their minds on the things of the Spirit" (Romans 8:5 ESV).

One's life is filled with emptiness when you consider worldly things as important. Don't allow people, or media, to choose your focal point in life. Don't let situations influence the direction in which your attention flows. Allow God alone to influence your attention and heart.

> "Set your mind on things that are above, not on things that are on earth" (Colossians 3:2 ESV).

A Christ-centred life is a life filled with peace, blessing, overflow, and strength. When things seem really challenging, your focus on the Lord will provide the peace, courage, and faith, you need to remain standing after the chaos has passed. God will never leave you nor forsake you.

I keep mentioning:

- To focus on Jesus;
- To focus on the Lord;
- To focus on God.

What does this mean? Look at the next scripture.

> "Finally, brothers, whatever is true, whatever is honourable, whatever is just, whatever is pure, whatever is lovely, whatever is commendable, if there is any excellence, if there is anything worthy of praise, think about these things" (Philippians 4:8 ESV).

These are only some of the things to turn your attention to. Truth, honour, justice, purity, love, excellence, forgiveness, gentleness, kindness, goodness, self-control, wisdom, patience, and mercy, are the things we should meditate on. These are the things of God. To be Christ-like, means to develop a godly nature, the character of the Lord Jesus Christ.

> "No one can serve two masters, for either he will hate the one and love the other, or he will be devoted to the one and despise the other. You cannot serve God and money" (Matthew 6:24 ESV).

Your focus cannot be on both your old ways, and the new person you are trying to become. If you are not ready to turn away from the things God is displeased with, recognize it, and know it. People with one foot in the world of wrong doings, so to speak, and one foot on the right path, are making life really hard for them-selves. Either you are ready to change completely, or you are not.

When it comes to turning your life around, it cannot be done reluctantly. Either you are fully committed, or you are not! Don't be fooled by assuming only some changes apply to you, and the rest of your old ways are still acceptable. You might get away with this notion for a little while, but it won't last. God is in the transformation business. If you are renovating a house, you want to renovate the entire house otherwise it will seem unbalanced. The kitchen may be renovated and look new but the rest of the house is stuck in the past. Even though it takes time, it is not complete until the whole house has been completely refurbished. In this same way, God wants to renovate your entire life.

> "No temptation has overcome you that is not common to man. God is faithful, and He will not let you be tempted beyond your ability, but with the temptation He will also provide the way of escape, that you may be able to endure it" (1 Corinthians 10:13 ESV).

As you grow in courage to lay down the wrong things, and turn your attention to the things of God, He will direct and lead you. The enemy may at times remind you of your past sins. Remind Satan that Jesus already paid the price for your right standing with God. The Lord is with you, to help you overcome these battles.

> "Jesus said to him, 'No one who puts his hand to the plow and looks back is fit for the kingdom of God'." (Luke 9:62 ESV)

Don't keep looking back when you are moving forward. The past is behind you. Your attention and energy must be spent on the things that lay ahead you. God is in your present and future, as long as you choose to place Him there.

> "Let your eyes look directly forward, and your gaze be straight before you" (Proverbs 4:25 ESV).

If you focus on the past, you will live in the past. If you focus on today and tomorrow, you will live today and plan for tomorrow. When people remind you of your past, then they are stuck in their own past. They are still living there; – don't let them pull you back there. With God's help and love, influence people in such a way, that it pulls them out of their past and into today, where it is a better and brighter reality to live in.

The Lord is crying out for us to move forward into our purpose and destiny with Him. Satan likes to see us stuck in one place, and he likes it even more when we are stuck in a valley of despair. You are powerless if you are living in the past.

Let the Lord lead you out of your valley, and onto the mountain where you can feel the sun on your face, where you can find joy and peace with Him. Let Him show you your true value and significance. The Lord will never lie to you, or set you up for destruction. Lies, deception, and destruction, are Satan's intentions for us. God's intention for us is love, truth, and the empowerment of the saints.

Your challenge for this Chapter:

- Make a list of the things you keep yourself busy with during the week?

- Out of this list, which of these are the wrong things that tie up your day?

- How much of time have you lost while focusing on the wrong things?

- Out of your first list, write down those things that are good?

- How much time do you spend thinking about these good things, and what amount of energy do you put into them?

- Write down how all this is currently influencing your life and the lives of those around you?

- What do you think needs to change regarding your focus points?

All of these challenges are to help you find out what you pay most attention to. Pretty quickly you will be able to see the bigger picture, and be able to pin-point what gets most of your attention at this time in your life. It is up to you to decide what is important to you right now, but keep in mind, God knows the plans He has for you.

Here is a tip - If you don't know what you should be focusing on, start spending time with God. Find out. Ask people to pray with you if you don't know. If you do know, ask people to pray with you any-way. A good starting point is to focus on God's intentions, and work on how to develop a Christ-like character. Don't look at what others are doing, but look at what God is showing you to work on.

CHAPTER 25

Choices

The power to choose a life of excellence.

Every day we are faced with choices. The Lord Jesus Christ had to make a decision daily to serve and to love people. Each day He chose not to live as a King, but to live as a servant and an ordinary man. Daily He chose to follow the will of the Father and not His own will.

The Lord's discipline and obedience to God the Father is astounding. With excellence, Jesus was committed to the purpose He was born to. The Lord shared the following regarding *choices.*

Choices - The power to choose a life of excellence.

- What kind of choices do we make throughout life?
- Do we make decisions at all, or do we procrastinate and let it pass?
- Are we afraid to make choices?
- Do we make decisions based on people's input or opinions?
- Can we make our own choices without being influenced by external pressures?
- Are the decisions we make, only made to satisfy our own will, or do they involve God's will?
- Do our choices support a life of excellence?

- Do our decisions support goodness, or rebellion and evil?
- Do we make self-centred decisions? Do these decisions only involve our well-being, and serve our own ego?

It takes an honest heart to look at your life and how you decide to find happiness, joy, and love, within yourself. You always have a choice in what you decide to do.

What do I decide to do or say on a daily basis? Once we come before God, we won't be able to point fingers at other people for the choices we have made. Peer pressure cannot be blamed, and neither can we conjure up any other excuses to render ourselves blameless. The Lord has granted us the freedom to make our own decisions. He wouldn't force you into any situation. He wouldn't even force you into His way of thinking.

> "I call heaven and earth as witnesses today against you, that I have set before you life and death, blessing and cursing; therefore choose life, that both you and your descendants may live;" (Deuteronomy 30:19 NLT)

Some people are afraid of making a choice. They may fear making the wrong decision. Perhaps they were manipulated for a long time by people close to them. Their confidence in decision-making might be damaged as they may have been ridiculed, experienced emotional abuse, or were physically abused.

The hurt that some people carry is so unbearable and deep, that the heaviness keeps them in the pit of despair. As long as the *victim* chooses to keep this hurt alive, they give it a crippling power over their heart and mind. Once they decide to shed this crippling power and hand it over to Jesus, their healing will start. How can a wound heal if the thorn has not been removed first? Once that thorn has been loosened and removed and handed over to the greatest 'Surgeon', the wound can be treated with care and love.

Jesus is the one who starts and completes the healing process for you through the Holy Spirit. Once the wound is closed, the pain leaves forever. The scar may remain, but only as a reminder of the Lord's love, grace, kindness, and faithfulness, in bringing permanent recovery to the trauma.

The individual may also fear taking the responsibility for the outcome of the decision. When people are not allowed to make mistakes, and are ridiculed for making a wrong choice, they will think twice about standing up to make a decision. They may even choose to run away from making choices.

When a person is guided through their wrong choices and given another chance, they will not fear to try and make better choices the second time around. When they learn from the outcome, they will most likely make the better choice next time round.

We can only make good choices based on what we have learned. If tragedy strikes in our lives, or we are placed in disastrous situations we had never faced before, we try to make the best decision we can. At times when we face these frightening moments, we may make an incorrect choice, but the Lord's grace is sufficient for that moment. The lessons learnt will cause wisdom and understanding to grow inside of you, regardless of the outcome. It's what we call experience.

> "But seek first the kingdom of God and His righteousness, and all these things will be added to you" (John 8:38 NLT).
>
> "For whoever does the will of My Father in Heaven is My brother and sister and mother" (Matthew 12:50 NLT).

Jesus only made decisions that were in line with the will of our heavenly Father. The reason Jesus was able to do this, was that He had spent time in scriptures, reading God's word. Proverbs in the Bible is a very good place to start regarding choices and ways of living. Spend time in these chapters and let the word transform the way you think and make choices daily.

When we choose to love ourselves and choose to believe the very best for our lives, we become alive to the purpose we were created for.

Are you just living or are you alive? Living, for some people, means you are just going through the motions day by day, but living as though you are life itself, means you are alive, burning with inspiration, passion, and excitement, for each day.

If you are someone who sets goals to reach your dreams, go one step farther. Set standards in your life while you are setting these goals. Firstly, pursue excellence in your relationship with God, then it will naturally manifest in other areas of your life. God's support is crucial when pursuing your goals, – you cannot achieve them alone.

Set the bar high. See what your best is. Stretch yourself. Don't fear your limitations. You might just surprise yourself, and even if you fail, move on. Try something new.

Your challenge for this Chapter:

- Looking back on your life, were there any choices you made that you wish you had made differently?

- How would you improve the way you are making decisions now, knowing that you are responsible for your own choices?

- Are you comfortable about making choices, or do you fear it? If you fear it, why? (Ask the Lord to bring the revelation to you regarding this.)

- Do you include God in your decision-making on a daily basis, only once in a while, or never?

- How would you change your choices so that you can experience more joy and peace in your life?

- What decisions would you allow in your life, so you can live with more purpose and excellence?

All of these challenges are to help you find out how choices caused you to end up where you are in your life. What we choose to do and say, may end up hurting and destroying us. The Lord wants to be part of your decision-making. He wants you to experience a beautiful life filled with happiness, freedom, and peace. We only make the right decisions when we allow the Lord to lead us in the right direction.

Humanity gets distracted by the world's standards and notions of 'a good life'. This tends to blind us from the truth, and causes confusion and fear, – two things that the Lord doesn't function in, which leads to destructive choices.

Here is a tip - Ask the Lord to reveal the answer to you. Surround yourself with godly people whom you know have a true relationship with the Lord. They can be a guiding light to you when you are facing difficult circumstances.

CHAPTER 26

Dreams

The power to change God-given dreams into reality.

Dreaming is one of the most powerful mechanisms for hope and purpose. The Lord had a vision of a changed humanity. He dreamed of a Jewish people that would come to know His great love for them. He dreamed of humanity being free from sin, and no separation from Father God. Jesus dreamed of a restored relationship between God and His people.

The Lord had a great vision. What is your vision? With this wonderful vision living in the Lord's heart, He had the immense faith to see it become a reality. He also had the discipline, obedience, courage, and patience, to see it through. Jesus had the right relationship with God the Father, to live this vision and purpose set before Him. The Lord shared the following regarding *dreams and visions.*

Dreams - The power to change God-given dreams into reality.

- What kind of dreams do we pursue?
- What vision are we following? Do we believe in this vision?
- How are we going to make this dream possible?
- Do we have immense faith in seeing our dreams become a reality?

- Are we afraid to dream?
- Who do we allow to influence this dream?

To have visions and dreams for your life is important. It brings direction and purpose to your life. We are not randomly born into society. We are not meant to walk around on this blue and green globe just because it happened to be that way.

Every life has been planned ahead of time by God. Even Jesus Christ's purpose was designed before time itself. Each person is spoken into existence for a specific purpose. No one is an accident. No one is a mistake. God wouldn't have made the effort of creating you, if He thought your existence would be a waste of time and reason. Remember, once you have been created in spirit and in truth, you will exist for eternity; – your life isn't going to end here on earth. It will continue into eternity.

> "You are worthy, O Lord, to receive glory and honor and power; For You created all things, and by Your will they exist and were created" (Revelation 4:11 NKJV).

Only God can create. There is no other being that has this divine power. If this is true, which we have just seen in scripture, your purpose is not just earth-bound, but will continue in the hereafter. The book of Revelation speaks about life after earth. Your gifts and talents go with you to heaven, where you will continue using them to glorify God. Therefore, the sooner you figure out your vision for your life, the better. You don't want to end up in heaven, hearing God say: "Well, while you were alive you were supposed to have done the following..."

How many people may have lost a blessing that could have enriched their life, just because you refused to be yourself and live your designed purpose in a God-given way?

We underestimate our value. The enemy makes it his eternal mission to persuade you of the following:

- you are a mistake;
- you add no value;
- you are not capable of doing anything;
- you are not qualified;
- you have no purpose for existing;
- you are damaged goods;
- you are weak;
- you come from a bad background or useless family;
- you are ugly and fat;
- your existence makes no difference;
- and many more...

These accusations sound familiar, right? And that is all they are, – accusations. They are not the truth. None of these accusations have anything to do with being able to have a vision for your life. None of them can determine whether or not you are capable of bringing your dreams into reality. The Lord placed the desire in your heart. He will help you achieve it.

> "He gives power to the weak, and to those who have no might He increases strength" (Isaiah 40:29 NKJV).

The enemy will use anything to stop you from living the life God had ordained for you. He will try to use people, situations, and even substances. Why? The enemy understands what a threat you are once you realize the reason for your existence. The very reason for your existence is to glorify God, and the enemy dislikes this tremendously.

Your life, gifts, and talents, glorify God. The beauty you carry in your heart magnifies the Lord, because He placed it inside of you. We are created in the image of God, and Satan despises this. When he looks at us, we are a reminder of almighty God and His promise to us.

Choose to pursue these dreams the Lord placed in your heart.

Don't place blame on whatever reason you may have, for not following your vision. Take responsibility for your future.

The same principle applies to our happiness. People find scapegoats in whatever form, to justify why they can continue living miserable lives and not be happy. The truth is that you alone have the choice to be happy. Only you can choose to pursue your dreams that will bring you joy, – regardless of whether you succeed, or fail, time and time again. When God is part of your dreams, you can be well assured that He is quite capable of assisting you in making it happen.

Wonderful things never come easy. There is always a price to pay. You need to be willing to fight and sacrifice. There is no room for doubt, jealousy, deception, stubbornness, or fear. Allow God to stand with you, and the blessing will be there.

Joseph is a good example in the Bible. He had many dreams of becoming a leader. Joseph had dreams of greatness. He even dreamed that all his brothers would bow before him, one day. Their jealousy came against Joseph, leading to his imprisonment and slavery. Joseph held on to his dreams, regardless of all the trouble. He remained faithful and loving towards God. Joseph understood who God was in his life, and he had a real relationship with God. In turn, God used all these situations, and turned them around to move Joseph into a role of leadership and power. Joseph never stopped believing and trying. He never sat in the corner and blamed circumstances. Instead, Joseph kept on serving, loving, and hoping. God honoured him.

Have you noticed that our dreams are very personal to us? That is how it should be. We need to respect each person's individual dreams. Whenever we can, we need to help each other in reaching those dreams we speak of. In doing so, God will send others to help you in reaching your dream, – you don't have to do it all on your own. The body of Christ is a gift to you, just as you are a gift to the body of Christ.

> "..., so now you must show sincere love to each other as brothers and sisters. Love each other deeply with all my heart" (1 Peter 1:22 NLT).

Avoid pessimists who only complain and get you down, regarding your vision. Only permit those who speak life and favour over your vision, to share in that walk, as it is a sacred and special walk. The road is challenging enough as it is. The Lord will send the right people to assist you in every season. Keep in mind, they too have a vision God placed in their hearts, whether their dreams are the same as yours or not.

In ministry, we use this approach, – to serve in other ministries whenever you can. To sow into other people's vision and dream, allows God to bless your own ministry with more than enough, – this is called the overflow. The overflow needs to be given away, so God can continue to bring overflow.

The other blessing that comes upon you when assisting someone else in their dream is the blessing of knowledge and experience. You will be learning some valuable lessons while watching different people pursue their dreams. This can motivate you, encourage you, and even save you from making wrong choices. As you see other people's dreams come true, your spirit rises with confidence that your dream is also possible.

Remember, these dreams should always be rooted in God. He alone created you for His divine purpose, of which come the correct dreams and vision for your life. If it is not rooted in Him, it may be that your dream comes from the wrong source, and could lead to frustration, desperation, and suffering.

In my past, I wanted to use sports to glorify God, but God had other plans. He had a greater plan for me, and allowed change to come into my life.

At the end of the day God was trying to tell me something: "Jeanne, you were dreaming too small. I want you to dream bigger. Your vision must be broader and higher."

Go for it. Don't be afraid. There is nothing to fear. See how far and how high you can go. See how much change you can bring.

Does your vision leave a legacy behind that speaks of who you are? If it does, what would it say about you?

Does your legacy bring life, hope, goodness and joy?

What would your legacy say about God?

Would it glorify God?

At the end of the day, it's not about your dream glorifying your cleverness and goodness (for most people this is hard to hear). It is about God's plan revealed through you, – Him using your life to bring glory to heaven and earth for God. What a privilege and an honour it is. King David's life glorified God. Paul's life glorified God. Let your life glorify Him too.

Your challenge for this Chapter:

- Write down your most important dream or vision. (If you don't have one, spend some time with the Lord to show you what your purpose is. This is very important.)

- What dreams or visions have God helped you achieve in the past? Thank Him for these.

- What dreams have failed, and do you know why?

- Are you dreaming too small?

- Who can you trust with your vision?

- Who can you help regarding their vision? And how can you assist them?

All of these challenges are to help you find out how your purpose and dreams line up within the will of God. When answering these questions, ask yourself if your dream will leave a lasting legacy behind, when you are no longer here. Or, will your dream and its influence end when your life ends here on earth?

Your life can make a difference to so many people, if you choose for it to make a difference.

Here is a tip - Spend time with people who are pursuing their own dream or vision. Learn from them. Pray about your vision. It all starts with prayer. Let God help you. Let His Holy Spirit lead you in every step and in every decision. He will not disappoint you.

CHAPTER 27

One Life

Why would you want to change?

"Why would you want to change?" – It's a very good question. You have every right to ask this question. But let us change the question around a bit. Why would you want other people to change?

You may want people to be more of the following towards you:

- Loving and accepting.
- Show you forgiveness and mercy when you have done them wrong.
- Gentle and sensitive.
- Soft and tender-hearted.
- Value and cherish you, – show their appreciation of you.
- Good and kindhearted.
- Have grace towards you in difficult situations.
- Listen to what you say, – pay attention to you.
- Understand you better.
- Show some interest in your life and what matters to you.
- Believe in you.
- Make time for you.
- Remember you.
- Offer help and support when you need it.

- Be happy for you and be happy with you, when it is going well.

Now let me ask this, "Can you offer the same change in yourself?" This is where the question comes in, "Why would I want to change?" Who wouldn't want to change for the better, if it meant it would change those around them for the better too!

It is a privilege to be alive. It is a privilege to love, to be kind, to give, to experience goodness, to give forgiveness, and to receive forgiveness. It is a privilege to be valued and cherished. It is a privilege to experience mercy and grace, especially when we don't deserve it.

I would rather want to know I have impacted lives around me with life, by being an example, - never forcing someone to be like me, but inspiring them to be like Jesus. Just as you and I cannot hold other people responsible for our own decisions, you and I cannot be held responsible for their decisions regarding:

- The *words* they speak;
- Their *thoughts*;
- Their true *motives*,
- Their *actions* on a daily basis;
- Their *relationship* and growth with the Lord, and the people around them;
- Their living a *life of excellence* ;
- The things they *focus* on all day;
- The *dreams* they have, or don't have.

We have to take responsibility for our own lives. That is all we have been given the authority to change and build. The rest is in God's hands, and should remain in His hands. We can support, pray, or give guidance, as friends and family who care. Allow the Lord to be God in your life, and in the lives of others. He will always do a better job at restoring people than we ever can.

Life happens to all of us. Good things and bad things. What we choose to do with it is up to us. I believe we all want to be good people, - people of great worth. No one ever intends to live a life of destruction, hurt, and pain.

None of us would ever want to be known for the following:

- Cause of someone's heartache.
- Your actions cause people to fall, stumble, or do things that would hurt or damage them in the long run.
- Being aggressive, rude, vindictive, bitter, or obnoxious towards other people.
- Speaking about people to others when it is slanderous, critical, judgemental, or humiliating.
- Destruction of someone's dreams through jealousy, envy, or greed.

When your attention is no longer on yourself and what you can gain from life, and you start focusing on Christ, your life will produce goodness. You won't be able to help yourself but change. Self-centeredness has to die every single day. If Jesus was self-seeking, none of us would have been given the opportunity to be truly free and forgiven. We would have been lost forever, and would never have known the power of unconditional love. We would never have experienced the power of grace and mercy.

Rebellion and pride are two of the worst joy-stealing and peace-stealing attitudes known to man. Rebellion causes separation, distance, anger, and hurt. A good, peaceful life is not possible, when a person becomes rebellious towards love; towards Father God; towards the Holy Spirit; towards Jesus; even towards the people who love them. Change cannot happen if rebellion is present in our behavior and thinking.

> "Likewise, you who are younger, be subject to the elders.
> Clothe yourselves, all of you, with humility towards one

> another, for God apposes the proud but gives grace to the humble" (1 Peter 5:5 ESV).

Satan rebelled against God. His pride was the driving force behind his rebellious actions and motives. God detests pride in any shape or form, because it destroys love and truth.

> "Give instruction to a wise man, and he will be still wiser, teach a righteous man, and he will increase in learning" (Proverbs 9:9 ESV).

> "My people are destroyed for lack of knowledge; because you have rejected knowledge, I reject you from being a priest to me. And since you have forgotten the law of God, I also will forget your children" (Hosea 4:6 ESV).

God's word urges us to always remain teachable, so that pride and rebellion will not enter and take root in our hearts and minds.

You only have one life. At times, change may be painful, hard, and exhausting, but God is with you as you journey in becoming more like Jesus. This transformation promises permanent change where peace, love, joy, and strength will become a part of you forever. I would like you to pray the following prayer whenever you feel disheartened, alone, frustrated with struggling, feeling hopeless, or you are overcome with despair:

> God, I come to You today, with the hope and belief in my heart for what You are busy doing in my life. Jesus, You knew You couldn't do things without Father God, and so You knew how dependant You were on the Father. In this same way I come to You Father, to help me through Your Son, Jesus Christ, to uplift my heart and bring an excitement into my Spirit, for the change I should experience on a daily basis.

Lord, I bring my life before you. You know exactly what its content is. In Jesus name, I lay down the old ways and ask You to help me take up a new way of living. Lord, I realize it will not be easy, and at times it would seem that I may not be making any progress. When I endure and keep at it, I believe I will start seeing the change in my life.

Lord, I understand that this change will continue for the rest of my existence, so Lord, help me. Keep me encouraged to continue in this process. This is how lives are transformed, healed, and mended by You. You are my solid ground, my rock in the storm, my refuge, and my teacher. You bring favor and blessing over me, and when I follow You, all things become possible.

I pray that I will always remember this moment, so that each day, I will feel free to face the day anew, and lay all these things before You so You can help me daily.

Lord, You will help me with the words I speak, the thoughts I have, the actions I do, the motives in my heart, the relationship with You and with others, living my life in excellence, re-aligning my focus on You, and working towards those dreams you have designed especially for me.

I pray that I will respect myself enough to be patient with myself and others, understanding that grace, forgiveness, and love are needed for transformation to happen in my life.

Amen

CHAPTER 28

Humility

A lesson in humility.

Pride always gets in the way of experiencing and living in true humility. Pride has so many faces:

- *Spiritual and religious pride*: People who act so super-spiritual about everything that they actually push others away.
- *Self-centered pride*: Everything is about them-selves. These people have no time to really listen to anyone else, and don't show real interest in the lives of others. They view them-selves so intellectual.
- *Stubborn pride*: Individuals who don't want to listen to advice, or learn something new. To them their view is the only correct view. Everyone else is wrong.
- *Shameful pride*: People who are battling with something, but cannot accept help or assistance from others. They cannot move forward in life. Or, they like to remain in their comfort zone, even when it is bad for them.
- *False pride*: People who act with false humility.

> "In his pride the wicked man does not seek him; in all his thoughts there is no room for God" (Psalm 10:4 NIV).

> "Pride goes before destruction, a haughty sprit before a fall. Better to be lowly in spirit along with the oppressed, than to share plunder with the proud" (Proverbs 16:18-19 NIV).

To break the power of pride, means releasing the very thing that is consider most dear. Pride devalues others, and devalues the things we should appreciate in our lives. Pride allows us to be preoccupied with ourselves.

"Pride allows us to over-estimate ourselves, and under-estimate others." - Pastor Stephen Lamprecht (Little Falls Christian Centre – South Africa)

Humility restores the value of the once devalued item or individual. At times you may even have to lose your life, whether it is spiritual, physical, or both, to come to this realization.

Loosing oneself, is the best thing that can ever happen to anyone

"The best thing I've ever been delivered from is myself." - Joyce Meyer

I may have lost my life at one stage, but it was given back to me. When you lose what you thought was important, you gain something much more valuable, – a new life; a new purpose; a new you. My dreams had changed, my life had improved, and my health returned, all because I exchanged my desires for God's desires.

> "He leads the humble in what is right, and teaches the humble his way." Psalm 25:9 (NIV)

Humility goes hand in hand with a teachable spirit. You want to learn the truth and you want to change. Thus, your ears are tuned to God's wise instruction, whether it is through His word, or through someone sharing a word from God.

> "If my people who are called by my name humble themselves, and pray and seek my face and turn from their

> wicked ways, then I will hear from heaven and will forgive their sin and heal their land" (2 Chronicles 7:14 NIV).

The enemy tends to use pride to cause separation when groups of believers are together. 2 Chronicles 7:14 is so important, - this scripture speaks about the believers humbly approaching God. It also mentions we need to pray, seek God's face, and ask for forgiveness. No one is without sin. People cannot be ignorant in thinking that because they are spiritually educated in the things of Christianity, that they are now perfect, – when in fact, they are far from it. When believers remain humble before the Lord, and do as the scripture instructs, division will never have a chance to rear its head in the believers' relationships.

Some people can take years or maybe a lifetime to be set free from pride. Realizing and admitting there is pride in one's life, takes an honest, internal inspection of one's heart, mind, and motives. The Lord is the only one who can assist you in working through pride. The Israelites had their experience for forty years, in the wilderness. It wasn't easy, but it was possible with God's help. If they couldn't reach the satisfactory state of humility God desired, they would never have been able to receive the promise of entering the Promised Land.

> And you shall remember the whole way that the Lord your God has led you there forty years in the wilderness, that he might humble you, testing you to know what was in your heart, whether you would keep his commandments or not. And he humbled you and let you hunger and fed you with manna, which you did not know, nor did your fathers know, that he might make you know that man does not live by bread alone, but man lives by every word that comes from the mouth of the Lord. (Deuteronomy 8:2-3 NIV)

Humility can also be translated as *human limitations*. When we understand we are limited, we start to surrender our independence, and start depending hundred percent on the Lord. That is the way it should be.

Meekness is the only way to hear God's voice, and to really hear other people's hearts. God cannot use you if there is no humility. Arrogance repels people because it is not love. Humility draws people because it represents love. Jesus knew the value of humility. He practised it and He preached it.

> Have this mind among yourselves, which is yours in Christ Jesus, who, though he was in the form of God, did not count equality with God a thing to be grasped, but emptied himself, by taking the form of a servant, being born in the likeness of men. And being found in human form, he humbled himself by becoming obedient to the point of death, even death on a cross. (Philippians 2:5-8 NIV)

The Lord saves the humble from many disasters that may come upon them. We live in a world where terrible things happen to people, but humility arms us with unexpected protection.

> "Have you seen how Ahab has humbled himself before me? Because he has humbled himself before me, I will not bring the disaster in his days; but in his son's days I will bring the disaster upon his house" (1 Kings 21:29 NIV).

> "For when they are humbled you say, 'It is because of pride'; but he saves the lowly" (Job 22:29 NIV).

Humility can calm anger in an instant. True humility can even calm the anger of the Lord!

> "And when he humbled himself the wrath of the Lord turned from him, so as not to make a complete

> destruction. Moreover, conditions were good in Judah" (2 Chronicles 12:12 NIV).

We need to practice humility towards God, and towards each other. This will cultivate love. In turn we give forgiveness, kindness, and goodness, a place to grow permanent roots. Humility will always supply the balance needed between people, to bring stability in all relationships.

> "Likewise, you who are younger, be subject to the elders. Clothe yourselves, all of you, with humility towards one another, for 'God opposes the proud but gives grace to the humble.'" (1 Peter 5:5 NIV)

CHAPTER 29

Serving

When it is not about you.

Definition of servant-hood, according to the King James Bible:

- Servant differs from a slave, as the servant's subjection to a master is voluntary, the slave's is not. Every slave is a servant, but every servant is not a slave.
- A person who voluntarily serves another or acts as his minister; as Joshua was the servant of Moses, and the apostles the servants of Christ. Christ himself is called a servant.
- One who yields obedience to another. The saints are called servants of God, or of righteousness; and the wicked are called the servants of sin. That which yields obedience, or acts on subordination as an instrument. One that makes painful sacrifices in compliance with the weakness, or wants of others.

Servant-hood is not about you, and it is not about me. It is all about Jesus Christ. It is all about serving in the way Jesus had served God the Father, and others. In this same way, we will also be serving the Lord Jesus. We serve the Lord by practicing our gifts. We serve Him by serving each other. And we serve Him by obeying His will for our lives.

The Bible portrays Jesus as the most beautiful example of the ultimate servant. True leadership is totally linked with true servant-hood. If you cannot serve, you will not be able to lead other servants of the Lord. A leader always leads by example, so if a leader was never a servant, how can the individual lead by example?

> "For even the Son of Man did not come to be served, but to serve, and to give his life as a ransom for many" (Mark 10:45 NIV).

The Lord didn't just come to show us how to serve one another, but He also came to pay a price for our freedom.

> "O Lord, I am your servant; yes, I am your servant, born into your household; you have freed me from my chains" (Psalm 116:16 NLT).

We were slaves to sin, but Jesus paid a price to set us free from this slavery. He gave His life so we could be free.

> "You, my brothers, were called to be free. But do not use your freedom to indulge the sinful nature; rather, serve one another in love" (Galatians 5:15 NIV).

A servant is always in five places:

- In the house of his master;
- With fellow servants of the master;
- In the presence of the master himself;
- In town doing the master's business;
- Completing the tasks set before him by the master, wherever he has been assigned to do them.

> "But be sure to fear the Lord and serve him faithfully with all your heart; consider what great things he has done for you" (1 Samuel 12:24 NIV).

Are you the Lord's faithful servant? Are you a faithful servant unto others? Do you know how to be faithful in all that you do? You will never find a good servant doing the following:

- Misbehaving when the master is away;
- Attending to his own business when he is on an errand for the master;
- Causing division between fellow servants;
- Taking over another servant's assigned work;
- Pushing his duties onto fellow servants.

> "... to love the Lord your God, to walk in his ways, to obey his commands, to hold fast to him and to serve him with all your heart and all your soul" (Joshua 22:5 NIV).

There are no lazy servants, and if there are any, they don't last very long. They will remain stagnant, never getting anywhere in their lives, because life is hard for an unwilling servant.

> And you, my son Solomon, acknowledge the God of your father, and serve him with wholehearted devotion and with a willing mind, for the Lord searches every heart and understanding every motive behind the thoughts. If you seek him, he will be found by you; but if you forsake him, he will reject you forever. (1 Chronicles 28:9 NIV)

A servant, who does his work with dedication, joy, and excitement, will be noticed and be placed in higher positions. Your willingness to serve others will bless you and enrich your life. The Lord will always promote a good and faithful servant! God honours a servant. A servant's work and love will never go unnoticed.

> "God is not unjust; he will not forget your work and the love you have shown him as you have helped his people and continue to help them." (Hebrews 6:10 NIV).

> "Whoever serves me must follow me; and where I am, my servant also will be. My Father will honor the one who serves me." (John 12:26 NIV).

I have this saying: "You will always find me with the Lord and His people, busy doing His work."Be aware of your daily location and how you occupy your time.

A servant is never greater than his fellow-servants, and never greater than the master. When a servant functions in humility, the Lord God himself will raise the servant up.

> "The greatest among you will be your servant" (Matthew 23:11 NIV).

> "Each one should use whatever gift he has received to serve others, faithfully administering God's grace in its various forms" (1 Peter 4:10 NIV).

Gifts and talents are used to serve others. They enrich people's lives, because that is how they were designed by God. They were not just created for you to feel important, successful, or superior. Your gifts reside in you for the sole purpose to glorify God in service unto Him, and unto your fellow-man. May this final scripture burn with life in your heart and mind!

> Love must be sincere. Hate what is evil; cling to what is good. Be devoted to one another in brotherly love. Honor one another above yourselves. Never be lacking in zeal, but keep your spiritual fervor, serving the Lord. Be joyful in hope, patient in affliction, faithful in prayer. Share with God's people who are in need. Practice hospitality. (Romans 12:9-13 NIV)

CHAPTER 30

Glory

All for the glory of God.

All the chapters of this book come together in this final chapter. Having been given a second chance at life, I realized that my experience of heaven wasn't just to rectify my perspective of life and God. It was ultimately about glorifying God alone, through living His purpose for my life. In the past, without realizing, I was actually living to glorify myself, even though that was not my intention. Many people today are living in the same way, without realizing it. I hope that this truth may come to light for you in these last pages.

Glorious means:

- to be illustrious;
- to be of exalted excellence and splendour;
- resplendent in majesty and divine attributes;
- noble;
- renowned;
- celebrated;
- extremely honourable;
- great dignity.

The word glory, or glorious, is known for being used in the circles of royals and victors. It is a word mostly singled out to a special group of chosen people. It is a word to describe something, or someone, quite unique and wonderful.

In the Bible, God is brought honour and praise, but most of all, all glory is acclaimed to Him alone.

> "Yours, O Lord, is the greatness and the power and the glory and the victory and the majesty, for all that is in the heavens and the earth is Yours; Yours is the kingdom, and Yours it is to be exalted as Head over all" (1 Chronicles 29:11AMP).

Jesus Christ is the Son of God, and therefore all glory is due to Him.

> "So that at the name of Jesus every knee should bow in heaven and on earth and under the earth" (Philippians 2:10 ESV).

When Jesus was alive on earth, He brought glory to God the Father, because He understood the Father, and wanted us to understand the importance of glorifying God. Jesus did this by living out the plan God had for Him. In this same way, we glorify God when we live out the plan God has for our lives.

> "I glorified you on earth, having accomplished the work that you gave me to do. And now, Father, glorify me in your own presence with the glory that I had with you before the world existed" (John 17:4-5 ESV).

> "He is the radiance of the glory of God and the exact imprint of his nature, and he upholds the universe by the word of his power. After making purification for sins, he sat down at the right hand of the Majesty on high…" (Hebrews 1:3 ESV)

When Jesus died and returned to the Father, all glory was restored to Him. In the same way when we die one day, we will be completely restored to the glory which God has in store for us.

> "I am the Lord; that is my name; my glory I give to no other, nor my praise to carved idols" (Isaiah 42:8 ESV).

The glory of the Lord is so pure, sacred, and perfect, that it cannot, and never will be acclaimed by anything or anyone else. God is the very essence of glory. He is the source of glory. He is glory.

> For from Him and through Him and to Him are all things. [For all things originate with Him and come from Him; all things live through Him, and all things center in and tend to consummate and to end in Him.] To Him be the glory forever! Amen (so be it). (Romans 11: 36 AMP))

God's glory is so magnificent that it lights up the whole of heaven. God's glorious light is saturated with life, goodness, love, kindness, honour, dignity, nobility, and excellence.

> And the city has no need for sun or moon to shine on it, for the glory of God gives it light, and its lamp is the Lamb. By its light will the nations walk, and the kings of the earth will bring their glory into it, and its gates will never be shut by day – and there will be no night there. (Revelation 21:23-25 ESV)

Imagine, this same glory of almighty God coming to stay inside of you, and then transforming you from glory to glory. This is what happens with someone who surrenders his life to Jesus Christ. He becomes a believer. He then starts living according to God's word.

> "But glory and honor and [heart] peace shall be awarded to everyone who [habitually] does good, the Jew first and also the Greek (Gentile)..." (Romans 2:10 AMP)

> "So, whether you eat or drink, or whatever you do, do all to the glory of God" (1 Corinthians 10:31 ESV).

In whatever we do, let us do it unto the Lord as to glorify Him. If we represent the Lord in this world, we need to bring honour and glory to the meaning of who He is. If you are in the air-force for example, and you are wearing your uniform in public, you are expected to act a certain way. Your behavior, your words, and your actions, will be a reflection on the air-force. The way you conduct yourself, has to be in line with the uniform you are wearing.

The same goes for us as believers. We will only be known as God's children when our behavior is in line with God's nature. When our conduct is out of line, and people know you are a Christian, they will question God's nature at the same time.

"Why would I want to be a Christian if this is the way they act?" I have heard this statement, time and time again. I had the unfortunate experience of witnessing how a so-called 'Lady of a Church', ended up swearing and cursing a bank teller one morning. Then after the church lady left, I overheard a stranger comment, "And she carries a bible under her arm?" This is a typical example of the damage brought upon the name of the Lord, when believers don't walk in the nature of the Lord.

> "Not to us, O Lord, not to us but to Your name give glory, for Your mercy and loving-kindness and for the sake of Your truth and faithfulness!" (Psalm 115:1 AMP)

Be very careful how you portray God in your every-day life. It is the first and most influential testimony people get to see. How it must grieve the Lord when He sees us misrepresent Him. If you had to send someone into a meeting you couldn't attend, you would send someone who would represent you best, right? The Lord expects the same representation from us.

How do you represent the Lord? Do you represent the very nature of the Lord, or do you represent the enemy? Do you represent an unclean person? Do your words, actions, motives, dreams, and vision for your life, represent the Lord?

> "Then the cloud covered the tent of meeting, and the glory of the Lord filled the tabernacle. And Moses was not able to enter the tent of meeting because the cloud settled on it, and the glory of the Lord filled the tabernacle" (Exodus 40:24-35 ESV).

The tabernacle was filled with the glory of the Lord, – which means it was filled with His exalted, excellence, splendour, divine attributes, nobility, honour, and great dignity.

> "Now the appearance of the glory of the Lord was like a devouring fire on the top of the mountain in the sight of the people of Israel" (Exodus 24:17 ESV).

The glory of the Lord manifests itself like a consuming fire. This holy and pure fire, will burn up anything unholy and sinful. That is the power of the glory of God. It is the purest form of God's presence. This glory produces light in which the enemy cannot reside.

> "Arise [from the depression and prostration in which circumstances have kept you – rise to a new life]! Shine (be radiant with the glory of the Lord), for your light has come, and the glory of the Lord has risen upon you!" (Isaiah 60:1 AMP)

When believers become carriers of the Lord's glory, they become carriers of this light. Whenever they are in the presence of evil spirits, or a person leading an unclean life, their light will clash and drive away the evil spirit, convicting the unrighteous. A believer wouldn't even have to say a word. The presence of Jesus living inside of them will automatically do the conviction.

> "For all have sinned and fallen short of the glory of God" (Romans 3:23 ESV).

We have all fallen short of the glory of God. However, Christ Jesus has come to restore all that we fall short of.

> "To them God chose to make known how great among the Gentiles are the riches of the glory of this mystery, which is Christ in you, the hope of glory..." (Colossians 1:27 ESV).

Christ that lives inside of you, the hope of glory. Jesus promises to restore us in every area, where we lack and fall short. He will come to heal the brokenness in us, so we can become whole and restored, lacking nothing. We know we make mistakes and have sin in our lives, but Jesus promises to set us free from this, when we accept Him into our hearts. He will take away the shame and judgment the enemy placed on us through sin.

> "Then shall your light break forth like the dawn, and your healing shall spring up speedily; your righteousness shall go before you; the glory of the Lord shall be your rear guard" (Isaiah 58:8 ESV).

The glory of the Lord shall be your rear guard.

> That the God of our Lord Jesus Christ, the Father of glory, may give you a spirit of wisdom and of revelation in the knowledge of him, having the eyes of your hearts enlightened, that you may know what is the hope to which he has called you, what are the riches of

> his glorious inheritance in the saints, and what is the immeasurable greatness of his power toward us who believe, according to the working of his great might that he worked in Christ when he raised him from the dead and seated him at his right hand in the heavenly places, far above all rule and authority and power and dominion, and above every name that is named, not only in this age but also in the one to come. (Ephesians 1:17-21 ESV)

Ephesians 1:17-21 is a blessing I pray unto you. Take it and make it yours.

***

I hope that at least one of these pages spoke to your heart. Know that God loves you. Whether you believe in Him or not, He has always loved you, even before you knew He loved you first.

Conclusion

The salvation road.

PRAYER OF DEVOTION

"Dear Lord Jesus, thank you for dying on the cross for me. Thank you for your amazing love. I repent of my sins and thank you for Your forgiveness. I also forgive in the same way, those who have sinned against me.

Lord Jesus, please come into my life and give me a fresh start. I believe in my heart and accept You as my Lord and Saviour. I believe that Jesus Christ is the Son of God. I believe Jesus Christ died on the cross for my sins and He was raised from the dead for my justification.

Thank you, Lord, for taking me in and not casting me away from You. Help me to live my life for You from this day forward. Amen.

***

THE ROMAN ROAD

Now that you have accepted the Lord Jesus Christ into your heart and into your life, go and read these scriptures, as they will explain to you what the Bible says about Jesus, and being born again into His Kingdom.

- Acts 17:24-28 (explains who God is)
- Genesis 1:31
- Genesis 2:17
- Genesis 3:15-17
- Romans 3:9-12
- Romans 3:23
- Romans 5:12
- Romans 6:23
- Romans 5:8
- Romans 10:9-10, 13
- Romans 8:1
- Acts 2:38-39
- Acts 3:19
- 2 Peter 3:9

You can also pray Psalm 51

***

FINALLY

Jesus has now washed your sins away. They are erased. (Read Isaiah 43:25) When we come to God as sinners, all that we have ever done in the past is wiped out, and all that we have ever been is wiped out.

You are a new creation. It is a new start for your life. Start reading the Bible. Find a good church, one based on God's Word and His Holy Spirit, if you are not yet part of a church. Start praying to the Lord, have conversations with Him.

Welcome to the family of Christ Jesus!
Remember you are loved!

www.ingramcontent.com/pod-product-compliance
Ingram Content Group UK Ltd.
Pitfield, Milton Keynes, MK11 3LW, UK
UKHW041945190726
13854UKWH00004B/1804

9 781490 869933